The Essential Guide to Teaching 14–19 Diplomas

Lynn Senior

Longman
is an imprint of

Harlow, England • London • New York • Boston • San Francisco • Toronto • Sydney • Singapore • Hong Kong
Tokyo • Seoul • Taipei • New Delhi • Cape Town • Madrid • Mexico City • Amsterdam • Munich • Paris • Milan

PEARSON EDUCATION LIMITED

Edinburgh Gate
Harlow CM20 2JE
Tel: +44 (0)1279 623623
Fax: +44 (0)1279 431059
Website: www.pearsoned.co.uk

First published in Great Britain in 2010

ISBN: 978-1-4082-2549-3

British Library Cataloguing-in-Publication Data
A catalogue record for this book is available from the British Library

Library of Congress Cataloging-in-Publication Data
Senior, Lynn.
  The essential guide to teaching 14–19 diplomas / Lynn Senior.
    p.cm.
  Includes index.
  ISBN 978–1–4082–2549–3 (pbk.)
  1. Vocational education--Great Britain. 2. Vocational teachers--Great Britain. 3. Effective teaching--Great Britain. I. Title.
  LC1047.G7S46 2010
  373.2460941--dc22
                        2010002736

10 9 8 7 6 5 4 3 2 1
14 13 12 11 10

Typeset in 10/12 pt Frutiger Light by 30
Printed by Ashford Colour Press Ltd., Gosport

The publisher's policy is to use paper manufactured from sustainable forests.

To my husband, Paul

Contents

About the author

Lynn Senior is the Assistant Head of Lifelong Learning Initial Teacher Training at the University of Derby. She has taught in the tourism, leisure, events, hospitality and food sectors predominantly in the further education sector but also in schools. She was initially involved in the development of a vocational leisure and tourism strand within the secondary PGCE course that was run by the university, but now spends her time working with the post-compulsory initial teacher training programmes.

Acknowledgements

Thanks go to my husband, Paul, for his love, support and for keeping me sane while policy kept changing. Also, to my fantastic colleagues at the University of Derby for proof-reading the manuscript and pointing out spelling errors with great enthusiasm! I'd also like to extend my thanks to all of the teaching staff who have provided input for the case study material, Heanor Gate Science College, 'Laura' for allowing me to use her profile as a learner and the Derby City Consortium.

Publisher's acknowledgements

We are grateful to the following for permission to reproduce copyright material:

Figures

Figures 2.3 and 7.2 Copyright 2007 David A. Kolb, Experience Based Learning Systems, Inc. Reprinted with permission from the Hay Group, Inc. (www.hay-group.com); Figure 6.1 from www.debonoconsulting.com/six_thinking_hats.asp, reproduced with permission from De Bono Global; Figure 7.1 from *A Handbook of Reflective* and *Experiential Learning Theory and Practice*, Routledge (Moon, J. 2004) p. 85, with permission from Taylor & Francis Books (UK); Figures 7.3 and 7.4 from *Learning By Doing*, Further Education Unit, Oxford Polytechnic, Oxford (Gibbs, G. 1988), with permission from OCSLD, Oxford Brookes University; Figure 8.1 adapted from *Everyone Needs a Mentor*, CIPD (Clutterbuck, D. 1985), with

Tables

Text

Qualifications and Curriculum Authority (QCA 2008) p. 3; Extract on page 64 from DCSF National Strategies website, http://www.standards.dcsf.gov.uk/national strategies, Crown Copyright material is reproduced with the permission of the Controller of HMSO and the Queen's Printer for Scotland; Epigraph on page 70 from *Quality Standards for Young People's Information, Advice and Guidance* (DCSF 2008) © Crown copyright 2008, Crown Copyright material is reproduced with the permission of the Controller of HMSO and the Queen's Printer for Scotland; Extract on page 72 from *A Short Guide to the Education and Skills Bill* (DCSF 2007), Crown Copyright material is reproduced with the permission of the Controller of HMSO and the Queen's Printer for Scotland; Extract on page 77 from http://www.excellencegateway.org.uk, © 2010 Learning and Skills Improvement Service; Extract on page 78 from 2020 *Vision Report of the Teaching and Learning in 2020 Review Group*, DfES (Gilbert, C. 2007), Crown Copyright material is reproduced with the permission of the Controller of HMSO and the Queen's Printer for Scotland; Epigraph on page 84 from *Personal, Learning and Thinking Skills*, Qualifications and Curriculum Authority (QCA 2009) http://curriculum.qcda.gov.uk/key_stages_3_and_4/skills/plts; Extract on pages 85-86 from QCA PLTS Framework, www.curriculum.qcda.org.uk, Qualifications and Curriculum Authority; Extract on page 93 from http://www.qca.org.uk, accessed 20/7/09; Epigraph on page 98 – this article was published in *Evaluating the Quality of Learning: the SOLO taxonomy*, Biggs, J. and Collins, K., p. 6, Copyright Elsevier 1982; Epigraph on page 112 from http://www.mentors.net, The Mentoring Leadership and Resource Network, MLRN/Mentors.net; Epigraph on page 126 from *Collaborative Learning Systems*, Nuffield Foundation (Hodgson, A., Spours, K. and Wright, S. 2005) Nuffield Review of 14-19 Education and Training, Seminar 2, Discussion Paper 10, reprinted with permission from the authors; Extract on page 126 from *14–19 Curriculum and Qualifications Reform: Final Report of the Working Group on 14–19 Reform* (DfES 2004), Crown Copyright material is reproduced with the permission of the Controller of HMSO and the Queen's Printer for Scotland; Extract on page 126 from *Collaborative Approaches to 14–19 Provision: An Evaluation of the Second Year of the 14-19 Pathfinder Initiative*, DfES (Higham, J. and Yeomans, D. 2005), Crown Copyright material is reproduced with the permission of the Controller of HMSO and the Queen's Printer for Scotland; Extract on pages 129-30 adapted from A Quality Assurance Framework for 14–19 Consortia, http://www.dcsf.gov.uk/14-19/documents/QA_framework.doc, Crown Copyright material is reproduced with permission under the terms of the Click-Use License.

In some instances we have been unable to trace the owners of copyright material, and we would appreciate any information that would enable us to do so.

Introduction

This text aims to remove some of the myths surrounding the 14–19 diploma and its place in the classroom. While, as with any book, it endeavours to lead you through the concept and implementation of the diploma in a logical manner, each chapter is written individually to allow you to dip in and out of the diploma aspects that you feel you need the most support with. I hope you enjoy reading it.

Recent history and development of the 14–19 diplomas

What this chapter will explore:

- Recent history of vocational education and training
- Discussion of the perceived vocational/academic divide
- Background to the 14–19 agenda in the UK
- Introducing the diploma and the lines of learning
- Who is the 14–19 learner?
- What are the issues surrounding the 14–19 agenda?

This chapter will explore the 14–19 agenda and the introduction of the diploma qualification, with an overview of the concept of vocational education and the learner you may encounter studying the diploma itself.

'Our aim is a system of 14–19 education matching the best anywhere; a system where all young people have opportunities to learn in ways which motivate and stretch them and through hard work qualify themselves for success in life; one where educational opportunity and chances do not depend upon accident of birth, but are uniformly available to all young people.'

(DfES, 2005, para. 1)

Introduction

The 14–19 sector and the new 14–19 qualifications have been described as a unique phase in UK educational policy and development (Lumby and Foskett, 2005). Let us consider some of the things that makes it unique and how they will impact upon you as a teacher working within the 14–19 sector. First, the new diplomas are based upon a consortia of different partners all working together to provide the elements of the diploma and the learning experience for the student. So who might be involved in the delivery of a diploma? It is envisaged that schools and colleges will work together to provide the major learning, but workplaces will also be involved as students will need to complete a work placement and in some diplomas an extended work project. This in itself is a major change for the UK in that not only do different organisations have to collaborate on learning and teaching, the different sectors are also sharing the students who choose to study for a diploma. For existing teachers it could mean that you may be dealing with students that you are not accustomed to, for example, If you work in a traditional post-16 college you may be required to teach Year 10 students and, vice versa if you work with Year 10 in a school you may suddenly find yourself with an 18–19 year old.

For a new teacher entering into the profession you will need to ensure that your learning and teaching strategies are appropriate for a much wider age group than you were perhaps anticipating when you started your teacher training programme. All of this could potentially be challenging for both new and existing teachers alike, not just the everyday dealings with the students, including teaching, assessing and ensuring that you provide an inclusive environment for them to achieve, but also to your school or college, which will need to accommodate a range of students and abilities. However, if we look at this from the learner viewpoint, our 14–19 year olds are in a unique and enviable position of studying both within the traditional 11–16 school and the less traditional further education college. If managed correctly, the best of both worlds!

In addition to the need for partnership working and effective collaboration the new reforms and qualifications also include an element of applied learning. In its simplest form applied learning is the learning, teaching and assessment of vocational skills within the classroom environment. If delivered correctly the skills gained from applied learning techniques are directly transferable into the workplace. To support this it is suggested that an additional partner is included in the school/college partnership, that is, the person still in the workplace, who visits to provide additional classes for diploma learners, for example, the hairdresser who takes one class per week but still runs his or her own salon.

In short the diploma has been introduced to enable the learner to gain the skills sought after by industry and in doing so create a better skilled workforce for the future.

| Why not try this? |

- For your given subject area make a list of all of the potential partners, both educational and work based, who may contribute to the delivery of the diploma.
- What work-specific skills do you think your students may need to better prepare them for working in the sector in which they are studying?

Recent history of vocational education and training (VET)

Despite the perceived uniqueness of the new qualifications within the 14–19 arena, vocational education and training as a concept is not a new phenomenon and has been the subject of educational reforms in many countries over the last decade, the rationale being that there was a 'perceived need for education and training systems to have closer and more explicit links with the contemporary requirements of society' (Chappell, 2001, p 22).

What is vocational education and how does it link into the new diploma?

Writing as early as 1996, Magalen defined vocational education as follows:

> 'All educational and instructional experiences be they formal or informal, pre employment or employment related that are designed to enhance the skills, knowledge and competencies of individuals ... whether these experiences are provided by schools, higher education, private training providers or by employers.'

(Magalen, 1996, p 3)

If we dissect this definition and apply it to what we already know about the diploma, applied learning, work placement, work projects, we can see that the new diploma has at its heart the very notion of a vocational experience for our learners. However as a concept vocational education has been discussed and debated in the British educational system for many years, with several reincarnations of vocational education and training being offered over the last 30 years.

The following initiatives are all examples of earlier vocational curricular reforms that were introduced between 1977 and 2004:

- 1978 Youth Opportunities Programme (YOP).

- 1982 The Technical and Vocational Educational Initiative (TVEI).

- 1983 Formation of Business and Technical Education Council (BTEC).

- 1984 Certificate of Pre-vocational Education (CPVE).

- 1986 Formation of the National Council for Vocational Qualifications (NCVQ).

- 1992 Introduction of General National Vocational Qualifications (GNVQ).

- 1993 Announcement of Modern Apprenticeship programme (MA).

- 1997 New Deal and University for Industry initiatives (UfI).

- 2000 Curriculum 2000.

- 2002 14–19 Extending Opportunities, Raising Standards.

- 2004 14–19 Implementation Plan.

To what extent have these reforms impacted upon your subject area and the qualifications you offer within your establishment?

What makes the introduction of the diploma different from any of these previous initiatives?

One of the things you may have reflected on is that the diploma is a mix of both traditional academic learning and vocational learning that in itself has been the subject of many debates over the years. The following section examines some of the issues and challenges surrounding vocational/academic studies that you may encounter as a diploma teacher.

The perceived vocational/academic divide

This text could echo many similar texts and writings that have been published over the last few years about the vocational system within the UK. Bond and

Wilson (2000) take the view that vocational qualifications are not robust and that a skills- and standards-based approach reduces the professional element of any given subject as 'propositional knowledge is prior to and superior to procedural knowledge' (p 136).

This viewpoint could certainly be one of the reasons why vocational qualifications are sometimes perceived as inferior to knowledge-based academic qualifications, in that they are functional rather than higher-level thinking skills which the learner achieves. Other authors talk about vocational qualifications being 'not for our children' (Jephcote and Abbott, 2005).

At this point it is useful to note that, historically, the UK educational system has traditionally seen 'a gulf between vocational and academic education' (Winch and Hyland, 2007 p 2). However, I would also point out that vocational education is perceived as being essential for the survival of the vocation itself and also of paramount importance to the country in which it is situated. To support this perception many authors suggest that within any country the economic performance of that country is ultimately connected to the skill level of the workforce (Marsick and Watkins, 1990; Senge, 1994; Garrick, 1998 and Boud and Solomon, 2001).

Why then is there a perception that vocational education is inferior to the traditional academic education?

One of the possible reasons for this perception could be as suggested by Coffey (1992), that post-war developments in education as a whole saw 'a vocational bias in the curriculum with explicit skills training for occupations appearing in the less prestigious secondary schools' (p 153).

Why not try this?

Revisit the elements of the diploma that have been designed to incorporate both academic and vocational learning.

From your experiences with a vocational curriculum and from your understanding of the diploma and the initiatives identified in the box on page 4, how would you ensure that the 14–19 diploma was not classed as an inferior qualification within the vocational/academic debate?

Vocational education and training reforms in the UK

As previously discussed the reform of curricula to support VET has been a key feature of the educational reforms within the UK over the last 30 years.

Student participation in VET within the UK has been growing rapidly since the introduction of the Increased Flexibility Programme (IFP). This programme was introduced in 2002 and aimed to 'create enhanced vocational and work-related learning opportunities for 14–16 year olds of all abilities' (DfES, 2004), and enabled 14–16 year olds to study vocational courses within a post-compulsory setting for part of their school week. In addition the reforms and expansion of the Modern Apprenticeship programme to include foundation and advanced levels has led to students progressing on to further and higher education courses within their subject area, leading to a *mélange* of age groups and abilities study-ing at both compulsory and post-compulsory settings, depending upon the subject and work-related skills being accessed.

So what does the new diploma look like?

The new diploma is being introduced in four phases, with a total of 17 subjects (or lines of learning) being available by 2013.

Phase	Line of learning	Year of introduction
1	Creative and Media, Engineering, IT, Construction and the Built Environment, Society, Health and Development	2008
2	Environmental and Land Based Studies, Manufacturing and Product Design, Hospitality, Hair and Beauty Studies, Business, Administration and Finance	2009
3	Public Services, Sport and Leisure, Travel and Tourism, Retail	2010
4	Humanities, Sciences, Languages	2011

They are being introduced at three levels, Level 1 – foundation (equivalent to five GCSEs D–G), Level 2 – Higher (equivalent to seven GCSEs A*–C) and Level 3 – Advanced (equivalent to 2.5 A levels).

Every diploma will provide an opportunity for students to progress, and there are several routes available depending on their starting point and their career aspira-tions. Possible options are shown in Figure 1.1.

So what are the components of the diploma?

The diploma is made up of three distinct components as shown in Figure 1.2.

● *Principal learning*, developing knowledge, understanding and skills in the context of a particular sector.

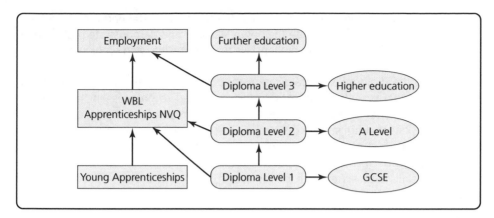

Figure 1.1 Possible progression routes for diploma learners

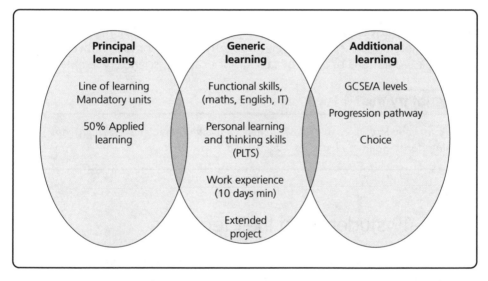

Figure 1.2 Components of the diploma

- *Generic learning*, including functional skills in English, Maths and ICT, and personal learning and thinking skills.

- *Additional/specialist learning*, which offers young people the opportunity to study a particular topic in more depth or broaden their studies through complementary learning. This will also allow a young person to create a qualification that is unique and individualised to their own specific career choice.

- *Work experience* is a key feature of all diplomas, with a minimum of ten days needed.

● *Extended project*: the diploma at Level 3 will include an extended project to allow individuals to plan and organise their own learning and demonstrate project management, synthesis and other higher skills that universities and employers need.

In summary the diploma is a qualification that combines both theory and practice to provide students with the necessary skills required to progress in their specific subject, or to enter the world of work. It has as one of its main components functional skills in English, Maths and ICT, and it will be a requirement of the qualification that students meet a minimum standard in each of these areas. In addition all students will participate in work placements where they will gain invaluable skills and experience of the workplaces and careers that they could progress to in their chosen subject area.

In order to create a package that provides every student with the opportunity to broaden their own personal knowledge and skills set, all diplomas will include an element of 'value added', additional qualifications or subject-specific learning which will personalise the programme to each individual. This personalised approach will provide students with the opportunity to build on their studies by taking a more specialist course relating to the sector, or alternatively expand upon their programme of study by taking, for example, science or languages.

Why not try this?

Look at your line of learning and identify possible additional learning that you could offer to your students as 'added value'.

The 14–19 student and their teachers

Can we define and identify who the 14–19 student is and what type of student is likely to undertake the diploma qualifications?

Why not try this?

From your knowledge of the 14–19 student make a list of characteristics that you believe they possess.

Did your list include any of the following – motivated, engaged, high achievers, committed, independent learners?

Many teachers tend to stereotype the 14–19 learner as being a low achiever, a troublemaker, disengaged and a constant problem in the classroom. Why do you think this is the case?

One of the key concerns for you as a diploma teacher is the level of challenge you offer to your students. It could be argued that one of the reasons for the 14–19 learner being stereotyped as a disruptive, low achiever is because you are not providing the correct learning and learning environment for them.

TOP TIP!

Think about your students. Are you 'dumbing down' because of your preconceived ideas about the student? If so your motivated, committed, engaged and high achiever will soon become disengaged, demotivated and quite probably troublesome! Likewise if you challenge and pitch effectively your disengaged, demotivated learner will suddenly become engaged with the lesson and subject. Who says a student who has been classed as low achieving cannot achieve if the conditions and learning are right?

It is important to consider what effective learning and teaching are when working with diplomas and diploma students. There are many models that attempt to define and describe effective teaching, which will be explored later in the text. However, as a starting point when considering diploma teaching one of the most useful models is that of Hay McBer's three measures of teacher effectiveness (Hay McBer, 2000), originally commissioned for schoolteachers but equally appropriate for those teaching within the post-compulsory (college) sector. Figure 1.3 shows the three main components of teacher effectiveness.

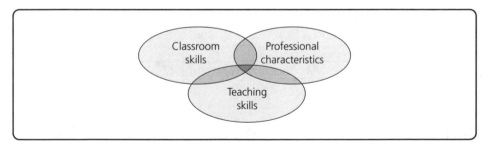

Figure 1.3 Hay McBer's three measures of teacher effectiveness
Source: Adapted from Hay McBer (2000)

Make a list of what you believe falls in each category. How can you ensure that you are effective, based on your list? A checklist based on McBer's research can be found in Appendix 1.

Reflecting on practice

Laura arrived at college with one D and a handful of Fs and Gs at GCSE. She was unruly, rude and quite frankly a pain in the classroom. Gradually, however, Laura started to realise that the applied vocational learning that she was experiencing was something that she could relate to, and while she still struggled with the 'academic' elements of the course, she flourished and started to get good marks. As the teacher who spent most of the time with Laura it soon became apparent that she responded well to *doing* things (kinaesthetic activity) and became more problematic when the activity was audio or visually based. In discussion with Laura a programme was designed to help her cope with the elements of classes she found challenging and extra support provided for her academic study.

Following her success on a foundation programme Laura continued in education and has recently graduated with a merit at Master Level, and now works in conservation. I for one am very proud of her achievements and Laura, herself a strong advocate of applied learning, says, 'the teachers wrote me off at school, I was told I would never amount to anything'.

Consider the following:

1. Why do you think Laura was 'written off 'by her schoolteachers?
2. What aspects of her vocational course do you think motivated Laura to engage with the subject?
3. Have you come across children with similar issues to Laura in your class?
4. How have you reacted to the situation?
5. How could you as a teacher help the likes of Laura? (Look at the McBer list to help you here.)

Teacher training issues and opportunities for the 14–19 diploma teacher

At the time of writing the 14–19 qualifications straddle two government sectors. The 14–16 year olds and their teachers have traditionally been overseen by the Teacher Development Agency (TDA), while the 16+ learner has a new sector skills council responsible for its workforce and students, Lifelong Learning UK (LLUK). See Figure 1.4.

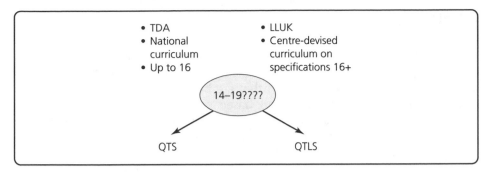

Figure 1.4 Sector skills councils and the corresponding qualification framework

This has been problematic for the workforce involved in the 14–19 diploma as the teaching qualification requirement for each sector is different, with the compulsory sector staff needing Qualified Teacher Status (QTS) and the post-compulsory needing QTLS (Qualified Teacher Learning Skills). If the diploma is viewing the 14–19 year old as a unique student, which teaching qualifications are appropriate and which body should oversee the delivery, TDA or LLUK?

If the diploma is to be a partnership of compulsory and post-compulsory teaching establishments should there be a third sector skills council?

Diploma challenges

As previously discussed, if the diploma is to be implemented effectively within our curriculum there need to be a number of different partners and stakeholders working together to provide all of the opportunities and learning experiences for our young people. This concept of collaboration and consortia is one of the key foundation bricks upon which this educational reform is founded. However, it does bring with it several challenges that need to be considered carefully if the qualifications are going to be successful and engaging for the learner.

One of the most challenging aspects of diploma development is that any one school is unlikely to have the expertise or equipment to deliver all the diplomas. So they are being developed by partnerships and will typically involve schools, colleges and perhaps employers working in collaboration. Students and teachers will have to be more mobile and flexible: travelling to different centres for different courses and/or working via information and communication technology. But on a far larger scale there are major issues of transport – especially in rural areas – health and safety, curriculum and timetabling, employment conditions and cost. This will be explored in more detail in Chapter 9.

Conclusion

The idea of a vocational curriculum and qualifications is not new. What is new is the use of partnerships to deliver an inclusive curriculum to meet the needs of all our learners. The new qualifications that are being rolled out from 2008 are a mixture of academic, applied and work-based learning, tailored to each individual through the additional learning elements that can be added to the generic and subject-specific elements of the qualification. As a concept there have been many different viewpoints surrounding the applied/vocational element and the introduction of the diploma will not be without its challenges in the years to come.

Key ideas summary

- What are the arguments for offering *all* young people the opportunity to become educated and skilled?

- How have previous vocational reforms impacted upon your subject to date?

- Should we perceive the 14–19 phase as unique?

- Is there such a thing as a 14–19 learner?

- Should qualifications be labelled vocational/academic?

Going further

Bond, C. and Wilson, V. (2000) 'Bridging the academic and vocational divide: A case study on work-based learning in the UK NHS', *Innovations in Education and Training International*, www.tandf.co.uk/journals (accessed March 2008).

Boud, D. and Solomon, N. (eds) (2001) *Work-based Learning: A New Higher Education?*, Buckingham: SRHE and Open University Press.

Chappell, C. (2001) 'Issues of teacher identity in restructuring Australian vocational education and training (VET) system', *Australian and New Zealand Journal of Vocational Research*, 9, 21–39.

Coffey, D. (1992) *Schools and Work: Developments in Vocational Education*, London: Cassell.

DfES (2004) *Evaluation of Increased Flexibilities for 14–16 year olds: The First Year-Brief*, London: HMSO.

DfES (2005) *14–19 Educational and Skills Implementation Plan*, London: HMSO.

Garrick, J. (1998) *Informal Learning in the Workplace: Unmasking Human Resource Development*, New York: Routledge.

Hay McBer (2000) *Research into Teacher Effectiveness*, London: Hay Group/DfEE.

Hyland, T. (2002) 'On the upgrading of vocational studies: Analysing prejudice and subordination in English education', *Educational Review*, 54, 3, 287–96.

Jephcote, M. and Abbott, I. (2005) 'Tinkering and tailoring: The reform of 14–19 education in England', *Journal of Vocational Education and Training*, 57, 2, 181–202.

Lumby, J. and Foskett, N. (2005) 14–19 *Educational Policy, Leadership and Learning*, London: Sage.

Magalen, L. (1996) 'VET and the University', Inaugural Professorial Lecture, Dept of Vocational Education and Training, University of Melbourne.

Marsick, V.J. and Watkins, K.E. (1990) *Informal and Incidental Leaning in the Workplace*, London: Routledge.

Senge, P.M. (ed.) (1994) *The Fifth Discipline Field Book: Strategies and Tools for Building a Learning Organisation*, Toronto: Currency Doubleday.

Winch, C. and Hyland, T. (2007), *Guide to Vocational Education and Training*, New York: Continuum.

Yan, W., Goubeaud, K. and Fry C. (2005) 'Does school-to-work make a difference? Assessing students' perceptions and practices of career-related skills', *Journal of Vocational Education and Training*, 57, 2, 219–35.

http://www.lifelonglearninguk.org/documents/Excellence_in_Supporting_Applied_Learning.pdf or hard copy (free) via www.teach14–19.org – 'Excellence in Supporting Applied Learning'.

http://www.lifelonglearninguk.org/documents/Training_and_Development_Guidance.pdf or hard copy (free) via www.teach14–19.org – 'Training and Development Guidance for Teachers of Diplomas' (aka 'TDG').

www.dfes.gov.uk/14–19/

www.teach14–19.org

www.lsc.gov.uk/Jargonbuster/Lines+of+learning.htm

Chapter

2

Learning and teaching strategies for the effective diploma teacher

What this chapter will explore:

- A brief overview of the range of learning theories
- Overview of learning styles
- Definitions of applied and work-related learning
- Discussion of the range of learning and teaching methods available for the 14–19 teacher
- Legalities of work-related/applied learning

Everyone learns differently and a vocational learner will have preferences for different learning styles and teaching methods exactly the same as a student studying for traditional academic qualifications will have. This chapter will review some of the key learning theories and styles. Further reading to signpost those of you less experienced within the classroom will be provided at the end of the chapter.

'Perhaps the one certainty about educational ideas is that there can be no consensus.'

(Halsall and Cockett, 1996, p 117)

I would start with the suggestion that it is important for any teacher that they have an understanding of some of the theories surrounding teaching and learning in order to be able to make the best choices when planning and delivering classes.

Several schools of learning theory exist that you may wish to draw upon when working with diploma lines, but regardless of which theories you favour you will need to have your own repertoire and bank of actual learning and teaching methods in order to cater for your range of learners.

Let's start by looking at some of the learning theories that you may wish to consider when planning and preparing for your diploma classes.

Learning theories

Behaviourism

The main concept underpinning the behaviourist learning theory is that the learner responds to a stimuli in a stimulus/response relationship:

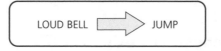

Over time the stimulus can be linked to new forms of behaviour, for example:

This then becomes a learnt behaviour, and a loud bell is associated with eating, you feel hungry. The learners are therefore conditioned to respond in a particular way. I use this as a concept in my classes to bring learners back together again following a group or individual task. For example, a simple switching on or off of the lights signals that I wish the group to be quiet, other noises and gestures signal other behaviours. A particular favourite with younger learners is the croaking frog. This is the signal that the time allocated for the group task has expired and we need to regroup and discuss. The frog itself is a simple wooden frog that allows you to create a croaking noise by running a wooden stick across the frog's back. Simple but effective, and just one of a myriad of props that you could have in your repertoire.

If we relate the theory of behaviourism, or behaviourist learning, to the 14–19 diploma and the wider remit of vocational learning we could perhaps suggest that using teacher demonstration followed by student copying and repeating a particular work-based skill would be an appropriate method to use within the classroom, as skills cannot be acquired without practice and the opportunity to 'get it wrong' in a safe environment. One of the most well known behaviourism theorists is Skinner (1904–1990), who developed the concept that behaviour could be shaped through positive reinforcement. For 14–19 learners, as with many other learners, encouraging comments in class are more likely to encourage them to become more involved with the task or problem. What is clear is that as a theory behaviourist learning is an obvious choice. For example, if we look at early child education, whereby rewards can be given for appropriate behaviour, and punishment for inappropriate behaviour, we are clearly using Skinner's positive and negative reinforcement strategies. It is also true to say that the act of repetition and active learning, or 'learning by doing', is more effective than passive learning

However as teachers do we need to consider how we test a learner's understanding of a particular skill if they have been taught through a purely behaviourist approach and conditioned to respond in a certain way? Consider: how could you ensure that your learners could explain as well as *do* a particular task?

Reflecting on practice

Paul assesses on the construction diploma. He is frustrated that during his assessment of learners they can quite often complete the task required of them, but are then not able to explain their actions, nor repeat them if slight changes are made to the assessment set-up. It is clear that they have been taught using the behaviourist theories of learning.

Consider the following:

How appropriate is this if the skills are supposed to be work-related and, more importantly, transferable to the workplace?

Cognitivism and constructivism

As a theory cognitivism seems to adapt a different stance from behaviourism in that it is concerned with the way people perceive and understand that which is happening around them and not just as a response to a stimuli. To apply it to a learning process cognitivism sees the learner selecting, interpreting and using the information available to them in order to create knowledge. Constructivist theory suggests that the learner then uses this knowledge and builds upon it to create a framework upon which they can further enhance and improve their knowledge.

If we consider our 14–19 learner, how can we best make use of this theory in our planning? One of the most effective ways to allow your learner to explore his or her knowledge and to build upon it is to use the concept map, developed from the original 'schema theory' put forward by Piaget (1896–1980). Piaget believed that when you encounter something new you either assimilate it into what you know already, or you have to accommodate it by creating new sets of information, such as opening a new file when you start a new subject. For example, psychology is a bit like sociology, so you will group the two until you know more about one or other. This new subject then needs its own set of information. The original theory suggested that human beings created mental maps to allow them to understand what was happening around them. For our 14–19 learners the use of the concept map can aid learning by allowing them to discover and make connections between any two points. Figure 2.1 shows a concept map that represents the impacts of mass tourism on a small fishing village.

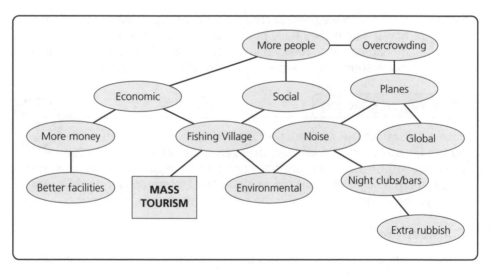

Figure 2.1 Concept map

Although this example is incomplete and many more strands could be added to extend the information, as a strategy the method can be used as an initial tool to create discussion amongst learners. It can also allow you to assess prior knowledge if done as a starter activity, provide you with an overview of their understanding of the topic if used as a plenary activity, and if used within the main body of the session can be used as a collaborative learning tool to allow learners to share ideas and add or build upon their original thoughts. Colour can be introduced to demonstrate different key points, for example the positive and negative effects or the different types of effect that the village may experience. If used throughout a programme of learning the student can add to it as their knowledge develops, making different connections and adding different areas for discussion.

TOP TIP!

As a learning theory I also find a concept map works well for me as the teacher, helping me to plan my scheme of work or lessons by allowing me to identify what must be included, what should be included, and what would be good to include time permitting (see Figure 2.2.).

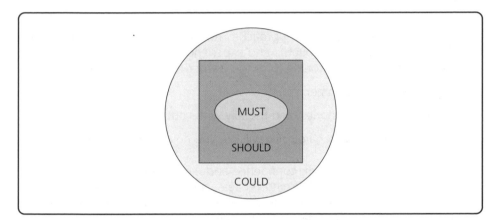

Figure 2.2 Planning cycle

Why not try this?

Look at the subject specifications that have been developed for your diploma line. Identify a module that you are comfortable with and create a concept map of the areas which you feel need to be included in the scheme of work.

Other theorists you may wish to explore within the field of cognitivism and construction are Bruner (1915–), who believed that learning is a social process in which learners construct understanding through interaction and communication. As a learning theory Bruner's theory has three main elements: the acquisition of knowledge, the transformation of knowledge and the evaluation of knowledge. He advocated the use of discovery learning as the most effective method to problem solving and as a method it is based on student-centred approaches in which the role of the teacher is to provide opportunities for learning. In other words, 'teaching by asking' rather than 'teaching by telling' (Petty, 2004, p 296).

Vygotsky (1896–1934) is a further constructivist theorist who is worth mentioning here, as his work revolved around challenging the learners to achieve by providing scaffolding to help them to progress. Scaffolding allows the learner to achieve in a secure and safe environment, but only if the teacher knows the learner and his or her ability. This is where the use of individual learning plans (ILPs) and the initial information, advice and guidance (IAG) plays a crucial part in your classroom activities. For more information on ILPs and IAG and how you can use it more effectively please look at Chapter 5.

Humanism

As a learning theory humanistic approaches remove all barriers to learning and replace them with positive thoughts and experiences. In essence the humanistic approach creates a safe environment for the learner to learn in, based on:

warmth (you feel welcome);

genuiness (people are honest and friendly with you);

unconditional positive regard (they will like you no matter how you behave).

This builds positive self-esteem, confidence and a willingness to try new things, where they help to drive the learning process, and can follow areas of interest. For your 14–19 learners this type of approach may be fundamental in your teaching and learning repertoire. Many 14–19-year-old learners may already have the psychological baggage of 'being useless' or 'thick', a notion not helped by some of the perceptions of vocational education discussed in Chapter 1. What then is the tool in your armoury here? Think back to Laura, our case study in Chapter 1. She arrived with an attitude linked back to her previous experiences, and for a while she was very challenging. However, the use of humanistic approaches (the creation of a safe environment, where she was encouraged to feel part of the group) and constant praise (which could also fall into a behaviouristic model) and the development of her confidence through using teaching and learning methods that she could relate to helped remove these barriers.

Why not try this?

Consider your teaching sessions. How do you create a safe and supportive learning environment for your students? What humanistic approaches have you used, or could you use to encourage the less motivated students to engage?

Learning styles

The term learning style is an umbrella term used within educational circles that covers a range of different ways in which people learn, or their preferred way of learning. If you think back to your schooldays, how did the teacher impart information? If I think about my school years aged 11–18, I seem to remember being told things and having to write them down. There was very little opportunity for me to 'have a go' at something or even watch a video about something. The nearest we got to a video was a history teacher re-enacting the Battle of Agincourt with a ruler! Consequently at times we were unruly, disruptive and no doubt a pain for the poor suffering teacher. My favourite memory is of spending one entire hour lesson sat under my desk playing cards, and the teacher in charge never noticed, she just continued dictating! So knowing a little about learning styles and preferred learning styles may, if nothing else, save you from 15-year-old poker players.

A recent survey by Coffield et al. (2004) suggested that there were over 70 different learning styles systems. However, most teacher training and continuing professional development (CPD) programmes tend to concentrate on a favoured few: Kolb, VAK, Honey and Mumford, and Gardner's multiple intelligences. Let's explore these and identify whether they are useful for the 14–19 learner.

Kolb

Kolb identified a cyclical four-part cycle of learning based upon experience and reflection upon experience, as shown in Figure 2.3.

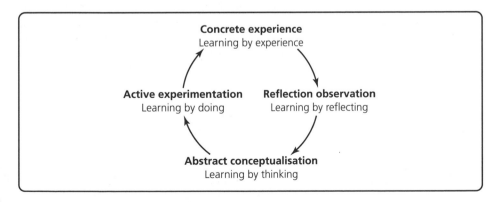

Figure 2.3 Kolb's learning cycle

Source: Copyright 2007 David A. Kolb, Experience Based Learning Systems, Inc. Reprinted with permission from the Hay Group, Inc. (www.haygroup.com)

As a theory of how people learn, this cycle would imply that your students will try something (useful for practical, work-related skills), reflect upon how it went, make mental adjustments and retry. For example, a student would paint a wall, think about how he or she had painted it, decide whether it was the best way and whether there were any other better ways of painting walls, paint the next wall using these ideas and see if it's better.

In an ideal world this is how we would all like our learners to learn: do something, think about it, decide if it worked, redo much better. However, does it take into account the frustrations and barriers that we know our students may have when the first attempt is unsuccessful? As a diploma teacher you will need to consider this cycle when teaching work-related or practical skills and assess how and if the learners progress around the framework and the steps you can take to reduce frustration and improve the learning experiences for all.

Honey and Mumford

Honey and Mumford (1986) take Kolb's learning cycle a little further and suggest that each stage within the cycle can be defined as a preferred learning style. They suggest that there are four different learning styles, each having its own characteristics and preferences when it comes to the classroom. The four styles are:

1. Activists.

2. Reflectors.

3. Theorists.

4. Pragmatists.

For you as the teacher, identifying the type of learner you are dealing with may help you plan more effectively and thus include relevant activities within your classes. The following table, adapted from Scales (2008), highlights some of the likes and dislikes of these four different learner types.

Likes	Dislikes
Activists	
Working in groups	Listening for long periods
Taking the lead in discussions	Note taking
New and challenging experiences	Following instructions
	Working alone
Reflectors	
Observing	Short lead-in time
Reflecting and thinking about tasks	Being put on the spot
	Deadlines on activities

Likes	Dislikes
Theorists	
Questioning	Unclear instructions
Structure and logical progression	Lack of structure to sessions
A purpose	
Pragmatists	
Links to theory and practice	No perceived benefit to the learning
Examples of good practice	
Guidelines	
Purpose to learning	

Why not try this?

From the above table, what personal characteristics would you expect to find in each type of learner?

How could you use this knowledge to help you prepare more effectively?

VAK

VAK (visual, audio, kinaesthetic) categorises the learners into three distinct types and is probably one of the most simplistic learning styles to use. It suggests that the Visual learner likes to see and use pictures and diagrams to help them learn. The Audio learner likes to listen, either to the teacher or to other auditory inputs. The Kinaesthetic learner likes to be doing, to be moving and to generally be active in a class.

TOP TIP!

A learning style inventory is quite an easy activity to do when you first meet your group. This will help you identify the types of learners you have and make appropriate decisions regarding the teaching techniques you are going to use.

See Appendix 2 for an example of the VAK questionnaire that you may wish to use with your learners. A note of caution here is that in reality we tend to be a mixture of the VAK styles, and although most people do have a dominant preferred style we must be wary about labelling our learners as just visual, audio or kinaesthetic.

Gardner's multiple intelligences

Gardner's multiple intelligences theory (1993) was developed out of a concern that most intelligence was measured on linguistic or mathematical capabilities. Gardner suggested that these two narrow definitions prevented some people from demonstrating things that they were good (or intelligent) at. Each of Gardner's types of intelligence again is linked to personal characteristics or method of learning. Here again we need to be wary as our learners may display a mixture of one or more of these intelligence types. However, it is a useful tool for any teacher who is struggling to get a particular idea or concept through to a group. While working with a group of 16-year-old learners in a school one of the group members was really struggling to understand a particular tourism concept. As the teacher, I had tried verbal explanation, visual explanation and collaborative practices, in the hope one of his peers could help him see the light, all to no avail. It was only when the class decided to create a rap song for part of their assessment that my learner had his 'eureka' moment. This learner is an example of someone with musical intelligence as defined by Gardner. Further attempts at engaging this particular student worked really well if music or chant (rhythm) was introduced.

See www.businessballs.com/freepdfmaterials/free_multiple_intelligences_test_young_people.pdf for an example of the multiple intelligences questionnaire.

Intelligence	Learning preference
Linguistic	Language, words, writing, speaking and listening
Mathematical	Patterns, problems, logic
Visual	Use of mental images and visual aids
Interpersonal	Like working with others
Intrapersonal	Reflective learners
Bodily	Movement
Musical	Rhythm, pitch
Naturalistic	Observing nature and environment

Gardner said that multiple intelligences were not limited to the original eight, and he has since considered the existence and definitions of other possible intelligences in his later work: spiritual/existential and moral. However, these intelligences are difficult to define and, not surprisingly, there have been many debates and interpretation of these potential additions to the model. It is for this reasons that you will probably only come across the eight listed in the table.

> **Why not try this?**
>
> Consider each of the Gardner's intelligences. How might you cater for them in your classroom? Identify one activity for each type.

Having explored some of the more well-known theories of learning and learning styles we now need to consider the diploma learner and the content of their programmes of learning. As we already know from Chapter 1, the diploma is made up of principal learning, of which 50 per cent is defined as applied learning, generic learning to include work-based learning, functional and personal learning and thinking skills, and finally the additional learning that creates the added value.

Applied learning and work-related learning as concepts are not new and the simplest definition is the application of theory into practice, that is learning the skills which they can then use in the world of work. However, with the introduction of the new diploma, the terms applied learning and work-related learning have suddenly become very mysterious and areas of challenge for the teacher involved in delivery. The next section will look at work-related learning and applied learning in more detail and attempt to unravel some of the myths and mysteries that appear to have developed surrounding them.

Work-related learning

Work-related learning is about preparing young people for the 'world of work' (DCSF, 2008, p 6). As a concept it is based upon the premise that schools, colleges and employers will work together to provide the learning that the student requires to improve their employability, enhance their knowledge of a given sector and allow them to make informed career choices. It should not be confused with work-based learning, which is learning in the workplace itself, that is students on apprenticeship programmes or NVQs who spend most of their time in the workplace participating in work-based learning.

> **TOP TIP!**
>
> Several resources and guidelines have been developed to help you navigate around what can sometimes be perceived as a complicated area: QCA 9-point framework, DCSF standards for work experience, resources from local education business partnerships (EBPs).

The DCSF (2008, p 8) further defines work-related learning as:

> *'Planned activity that uses the context of work to develop knowledge, skills and understanding useful in work, including learning through the experience of work, learning about work and working practices, and learning the skills for work.'*

From this definition we can clearly see that the underpinning element to work-related learning is that it is **F**or work, **A**bout work, **T**hrough work (FAT). So as a teacher how do we incorporate this into the diploma?

● *For work* is about developing skills for employability (here is where the application element comes in). These skills could be related to a specific work skill or could be much broader, e.g. interview techniques, which could then be transferable into any career area.

● *About work* is about providing opportunities for students to develop knowledge and understanding of the working environment through teacher inputs.

● *Through work* is about providing opportunities for students to learn from direct experiences of work, i.e. the work experience element of the diploma.

So what could work-related learning look like? Figure 2.4 gives you some idea of the types of activities that you could use to incorporate work-related learning into your diploma teaching.

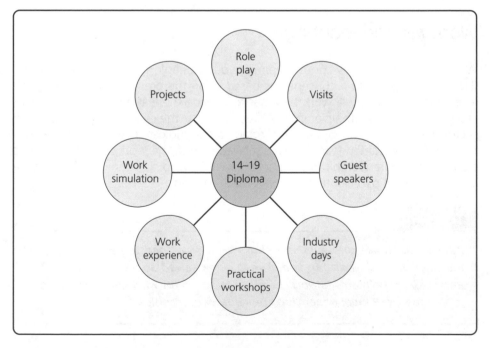

Figure 2.4 Possible activities for work-related learning

Why not try this?

Using Figure 2.4, what other work-related activities can you think of for your subject area?

So what is applied learning? Applied learning is a form of work-related learning and, while not all of the elements identified in Figure 2.4 can be classed as applied, the work-related learning that takes place in the classroom is the applied learning element. In its simplest form applied learning is the activities that do not rely on someone from the workplace to be present, that is the workshop, the role plays and simulations.

Teaching and learning methods for the diploma

Regardless of the qualification that you are delivering, an effective teacher needs to have a range of teaching and learning methods to meet the demands of a wide range of learners. As we have already seen we can base our choice of methods on learning theories and the learning styles of our students. However, as teachers we need to ensure that whatever methods we choose to employ in our classroom are methods that we are comfortable with and methods which suit our subject area. Consider the electrician who relies on PowerPoint presentations to demonstrate the correct way to wire a three-pin plug. There must be other, more appropriate methods that could be used for this type of activity!

The following list is by no means exhaustive but considers some of the techniques that can be used to incorporate work-related and applied learning into your classroom delivery:

- demonstrations;
- role play;
- concept mapping;
- discovery learning;
- problem-based learning;
- projects;
- presentations and marketplace activities (collaborative learning).

Lets look at a few of these.

Demonstrations

As a teaching activity a demonstration is a good way in which to show your learners a particular skill. In essence a demonstration is about showing another person how to do something.

Quite often teachers shy away from demonstrations because of their practical nature and the need to ensure that you have all of the relevant materials to complete the demonstration. This may be true for the Hospitality diploma, but consider some of the other subject areas. A skill within the travel industry is the skill of providing an accurate holiday costing for your client. What better way to teach this than to demonstrate on the whiteboard, allow the students to practise and then complete a role play or work simulation activity?

TOP TIP!

Do not make the mistake of thinking that to be work related a demonstration has to be practical. You can encourage the students to gain skills through the use of cognition.

Role play

As a technique, role play can be very useful when used correctly and, more importantly, if you have learners who are comfortable with role playing. Some learners may find the whole concept embarrassing and refuse to take part, while others may love being the centre of attention and be the constant volunteer. Think back to the section on humanistic approaches to learning: for many of your learners the role play may not feel safe. However, it can have its advantages in that it allows you to simulate 'real-life' situations without the risks that may be associated with the situation.

Reflecting on practice

During my time in a further education college I was involved in teaching criminology and disaster management to a group of Public Services students. One of the most memorable sessions was the murder crime scene role play. An artificial crime scene was set up and the students played the roles of forensic scientists and police officers. Fingerprints were lifted from possible murder weapons and the students had to discover who had committed the crime. Great fun: the students learnt valuable lessons about securing crime scenes without actually being in any danger.

Consider the following:

For your subject area when might it be appropriate to use role play?

Projects

Part of the learning for the higher-level diplomas is the extended project. There-fore at some stage you will find yourself working with learners on a project. What is a project? A project can have many different connotations, depending on the subject area involved. For the diploma learner it is the opportunity to demonstrate the skills and knowledge they have gained during the programme. It could take the form of a written report on a particular aspect of their subject or it could be more practical, say a video looking at a particular aspect of the subject.

TOP TIP!

Points to note for the project within the diploma:

It should be student led.

The teacher should be a facilitator.

The learners should carry out their own research, i.e. it is independent.

It covers an extended period, hence the term extended project.

Always check with your awarding body as there may be guidelines as to the content or appropriateness of certain activities.

Project work can be an excellent opportunity for learners to demonstrate the personal thinking and learning skills that are associated with diplomas.

Reflecting on practice

Zana is studying for a Level 2 diploma in Society, Health and Development. The following table shows what her learning will look like:

Principal learning	Generic learning	Additional learning
9 mandatory units	3 × functional skills qualifications at Level 2 (80 GLH)	GCSE Science
• principles, values and personal development		First aid at work
• working together and communicating	Level 2 project qualification (60 GLH)	
• safeguarding and protecting individuals		
• growth, development and healthy living	10 days work experience	
• needs and preferences	Personal, learning and thinking skills (60 GLH)	
• antisocial and offending behaviour		
• supporting children and young people		
• patient-centred health		
• the social model of disability		

Zana is interested in a career in youth work and is very interested in a project that looks at youth clubs in her local area. She is undecided what would be the best approach for her project work and has asked you for guidance.

Consider the following:

1. What types of activity would be appropriate for her to undertake?

2. What possible risks might be attached to the activities you have identified?

One of the things you may have suggested to Zana was a practical activity, looking at who makes use of the youth clubs and designing a campaign to encourage under-represented groups to join. Other possibilities could have been a written report on the types of activities that people wished to see in a youth club setting. Regardless of the suggestions that you gave Zana there are some guidelines that you may wish to consider for all project work:

- There needs to be a clear structure and focus for the student. Consider a learning contract.

- Regular progress meetings should be held between the teacher and learner be formally documented.

- Deadlines should be agreed to ensure that the project is completed in plenty of time for assessment.

- Study skills and research skills support should be made available for all students, both at the beginning of the project and throughout its duration.

Having discussed some of the ways in which you can bring your classroom alive and incorporate an element of applied and work-related learning, we now need to consider some of your and your institution's legal obligations when delivering learning in this way.

Legal considerations of work-related and applied learning

Some of the main considerations that need to be taken into account when delivering work-related learning activities are the rules and regulations which are in place to ensure that young people are protected during their learning experiences, both within the classroom and the workplace. These regulations include health and safety at work legislation, child protection legislation and data protection, to name but a few. The key point to note is that the school or college retains a duty of care at all times and should ensure that policies and procedures are in place for attendance monitoring, insurance cover, training and information for learners and parents, and vetting of work experience placements (including risk assessments). In addition colleges, employers and other training providers have responsibility for the health, safety and welfare of everyone on their premises. If we consider the diploma this could include a wide age range of students engaged in learning away from their normal educational establishment. It is particularly important to note that these responsibilities also stretch to ensuring that insurers are aware of the implications of their involvement with the 14–16-year-old learner.

Reflecting on practice

The local college works in partnership with several local schools providing vocational learning to Years 10 and 11 (14–16 year olds). Following a class designed to provide learners with the skills they need to work in the electrical and construction industry, the lecturer noticed that several screwdrivers had not been returned to the stockroom and that some of the practice circuits had been damaged. He made a mental note to report this to his manager and the school links person. Unfortunately events overtook him, and a student was injured when he touched a live wire on a circuit that had been vandalised by the Year 10 group. In addition the screwdrivers were found hidden in one of the teaching rooms.

Consider the following:

1. What rules and regulations have not been adhered to in this scenario?
2. Who should have ensured that the rules and regulations were adhered to?
3. What needs to be put in place to avoid a similar situation in future?

In summary the onus of duty of care needs to be considered carefully in work-related learning activities for the diploma, and as a teacher you need to be aware of the implications of not adhering to the legislation that is in place to protect both you as the teacher and the student themselves.

Conclusion

This chapter has examined some of the theories of learning and teaching that you could encounter in your role of diploma teacher. Some of these may be familiar to you, others may be areas that you have not yet considered. Regardless of your experiences in teaching it is likely that there will be areas of applied learning and learning in the workplace with which you are not as familiar, for example the legislation surrounding duty of care and health and safety, which as a diploma teacher you will need to engage with.

Key ideas summary

- How can you use learning theory and learning styles in your diploma classroom?
- What other teaching methods can be used to create reality in the classroom and how might you make best use of them?
- What risks are associated with your subject area?
- What laws exist to protect you and the learner?

Going further

Coffield, F., Mosely, D., Hall, E. and Ecclestone, K. (2004) *Should we be Using Learning Styles?*, London: Learning and Skills Research Centre.

DCSF (2008) *Work-related Learning Guide. A Guidance Document for Employers, Schools, Colleges, Employers, Students and Their Parents and Carers*, London: DCSF. Also found at www.dcsf.gov.uk/14–19/documents/work-relatedlearningguide.pdf

Gardner, J. (1993) *Multiple Intelligences: The Theory in Practice*, New York: Basic Books.

Ginnis, P. (2002) *The Teacher's Toolkit*, Carmarthen: Crown House Publishing.

Halsall, R. and Cockett, M. (1996) *Education and Training 14–19: Chaos or Coherence?*, London: David Fulton.

Honey, P. and Mumford, A. (1986, 2nd edn) *Manual of Learning Styles*, London: P. Honey.

Kolb, D. (1976) *The Learning Styles Inventory*, Boston, MA: McBer.

Petty, G. (2004, 3rd edn) *Teaching Today*, Cheltenham: Nelson Thornes.

Scales, P. (2008) *Teaching in the Lifelong Learning Sector*, Maidenhead: Open University Press.

→

www.businessballs.com/freepdfmaterials/free_multiple_intelligences_test_young_people.pdf

www.hse.gov.uk/legislation/hswa.htm

www.crb.gov.uk

www.doceo.co.uk

www.nebpn.org/cgi-bin/WEX_casestudysectorsearch.cgi – The National Education Business Partnership Network (NEBPN).

www.qca.org.uk/14–19/11-16-schools/index_s7-0-case-studies.htm – Qualifications and Curriculum Authority.

www.safelearner.info

www.ssatrust.org.uk/vocationallearning/workrelatedlearning/casestudies/default.aspa – Specialist Schools and Academies Trust.

www.teachernet.gov.uk

'Work experience: A guide for secondary schools'; 'Work-related learning and the law'; and 'Work experience and the law: The essential guide for central organisers, employers, schools and colleges' all available at

http://publications.teachernet.gov.uk – work experience guide for secondary schools

www.14-19diplomas.gov.uk

Assessment strategies for the effective diploma teacher

What this chapter will explore:

- Concepts and principles of assessment
- Modes and methods of assessment
- Assessing the diploma
- Overview of recording documentation

This chapter will explore some of the principles and practices of assessment and examine some of the tools that you as a teacher can use with your diploma students.

'It is almost impossible to describe curriculum and assessment separately: since the late 1970s they have been inextricably linked.'

(Haywood, 2007, p 254)

Concepts and principles of assessment

Before we start to look at assessment in any great detail we need to understand what is meant by assessment and why we as teachers need to assess our learners. In the world of education, assessment can serve a variety of functions and have several meanings depending upon whether we are the diploma teacher or the learner. For the teacher assessment can provide an overview of a student's progress, measure the distance travelled, identify any problems that the learner may have with a particular skill or area of knowledge, determine any issues that there may be with the curriculum and help you to evaluate how effective your teaching and the course has been. For the learner it can be a double-edged sword, inspiring, motivating and providing them with long-term goals and the determination to succeed in their chosen career path. However, it could also have the opposite effect if the learner perceives and equates assessment with testing and feels that the assessment was a negative experience, they were failing or not doing as well as they thought. So why do we even bother with assessment and assessing learners if it can have such potentially negative consequences? Talent, excellence and flair do need recognising, but this must not demotivate the weaker students.

Let's put this into context with the driving test, a test that most of us will recognise even if we have not had the pleasure of sitting it. The normal pass/fail rate is that 30–40 per cent of learners fail first time around, but the eventual pass rate is 95 per cent of all learners. What we need to remember when assessing our learners is that intelligence, aptitude or ability are measures of how quickly students can learn, not, as is often assumed, a measure of *what* they can learn. Consider the following two learners:

- Ruth Lawrence of Huddersfield went to Oxford University aged 12 to study maths, and gained the best first-class degree of all entrants in 1985 (aged 14).

- Fannie Turner passed her written test for drivers (in Arkansas) on her 104th attempt in 1978.

How do you think assessment affected them?

For all teachers, regardless of the sector in which they are working, assessment, or testing, will be an unavoidable part of the teaching role. Further to the reasons mentioned in the previous paragraph – measuring progress, identifying issues, motivating, inspiring and challenging – what we must remember is that most of the teaching and learning that takes place within the UK educational system is linked to the requirements of an external awarding body, or examination board, and the diploma is no exception to this. At the time of writing the main external agencies offering and conferring diploma awards are Edexcel and AQA/City & Guilds. These are the bodies which provide the proof, or certificate, that the learner has reached the required level of knowledge and understanding of the qualification specification. In addition, as they provide the overall certification upon completion of a programme of study, we as teachers are required to measure and test our learners against the standards of performance that they have identified within the qualification specification. It is our role to provide the proof that the learners have reached the standards set down by these external agencies.

Moreover, measuring our learners against the external agency standards also provides both us and the external bodies a measure of standardisation across the UK as all learners will be measured against the same outcomes. Failure to achieve these external standards could result in loss of funding to our institutions and in some cases we could risk our provision being closed down. Therefore, as a note of caution, we as teachers need to be careful that our assessments are not assessments for assessments' sake and that we are providing a broader learning experience, not teaching only what the student needs to pass. I always remember learning to drive and my dad saying you learn to pass and then you really learn to drive. Not something I would like to think I did with my vocational learners!

Before we look at assessment for the diploma itself it would be useful to recap some of the reasons for assessment within the diploma qualifications.

Checking learning has taken place

Within the diploma lines this type of assessment will allow you to check whether your students have mastered the new skill that they have been shown, or whether they have the ability to transfer their newly acquired skills and knowledge to the workplace. Actual methods of checking whether learning has occurred will be discussed later in this chapter.

Initial diagnostic of learners' needs

Many learners may have needs that you as a teacher must take into account when delivering the teaching and learning for a particular qualification. For example, a dyslexic student may need handouts on different coloured paper to that of his or her peers. Without initial assessment to determine a learner's needs a teacher and the institution may be failing their learners. In addition some learners may have difficulties or problems that occur within their personal lives which may impact upon their learning. You as the teacher will need to be aware of these issues to enable you to provide the support needed for them to succeed.

Initial diagnostic assessment allows the teacher to work with an individual student and to provide an *individual learning plan* (see Chapter 5), which takes into account both the needs of the learner and the requirements of the qualification being studied. It quite often assesses the level at which the learner is operating at any given point in time.

Diagnostic assessment can also be used to identify if the learner has any previous qualifications or work experience that you could credit towards his or her qualification. Within the UK educational system an organisation can use two different processes for allowing a learner credit or exemption for a particular part of the programme:

1. APL is the accreditation of prior learning and refers to learning that has previously been accredited or certified through prior qualifications.

2. APEL is the accreditation of prior experiential learning, or learning that has resulted from prior work or work experience. It would be unusual for a student studying for a diploma to actually have the appropriate level of prior work experience to gain APEL. However, there may be instances within your own subject where this could be possible.

Why not try this?

Consider your subject and the units within it. Can you envisage any instances where APEL may occur?

Evaluation of the programme

While we tend to think of assessment as being the way in which we test our learners, we must not underestimate its power in allowing us to test ourselves and the programmes that we offer. Using assessment as a way of monitoring what we do as tutors can allow us to identify areas within the programme that may need further development, or indeed to identify areas where we as tutors are not performing effectively. Many schools and colleges will measure the success of their students against the national benchmark figures for a given subject area. These benchmarks may be retention rates, pass rates, pass levels. We as tutors need to ensure that we are at least meeting these benchmarks or there could be funding implications for our institutions.

Why not try this?

Find out the national benchmarks figures for your subject. How do the results of your institution compare to these?

Motivating and inspiring students

This is where for tutors assessment becomes a cleft stick, for the learners the double-edged sword. One of the roles of the tutor is to motivate the learners through effective feedback and to build up learner confidence. Effective feedback is your tool to enable you to do this, through praise, recognition of work completed well and guidance on further improvement.

Negative, non-supportive feedback or feedback that lacks in developmental suggestions can be very de-motivating for the learner, and rather than having the effect of building confidence could lead to learners not trying or failing to submit anything rather than face what they perceive to be public humiliation.

TOP TIP!

When giving written feedback use the PIP method: positive, improvement, positive. For example: 'Joe, you worked really hard in this piece of work and have clearly understood the key elements of health and safety. However, to improve your grade you need to link the theory to your workplace to give examples that are relevant. Overall, well done!'

Why not try this?

Look back at the recent written feedback you have given to your learners. Does it follow PIP? If not, how could you rephrase it to ensure that you were providing your learners with effective yet positive comments.

Confirmation of qualification

As previously discussed, all diploma qualifications within the UK are set by the three main awarding bodies: Edexcel and AQA/City & Guilds, which at the time of writing are working collaboratively to provide the diploma. As these are the external agencies which provide the certificate confirming that a learner has reached a set standard in the subject, we as the teachers need to ensure that we assess our learners to provide the proof that they are competent and have gained the skills and knowledge laid out by the qualification specifications. As part of this assessment we will also be proving that our assessment systems are valid and reliable and that our standards are comparable to other organisations offering the qualification.

As part of this confirmation most organisations will require their teachers to hold a relevant assessing qualification and that all assessments are internally checked by a qualified internal verifier, who is also required to hold a relevant assessing qualification. Appendix 3 shows the possible qualifications for assessment.

Following this internal check work is then routinely sent to the awarding bodies for external verification, a final check that assessment is fair and that standards are comparable. As with other qualifications, diploma standards will be overseen by the new qualifications regulator, OfQual, which is accountable directly to Parliament.

All awarding bodies will have their own regulations surrounding the assessment process and internal moderation of work. The following box demonstrates how you can ensure that your assessments are completed in accordance with quality assurance processes, regardless of whether you need to send work to your awarding body or not. However, you must ensure that you check with your awarding body as this is only a guide and different awarding bodies may require different documentation.

Tips for ensuring that your assessment is quality assured

Every awarding body will have slightly different requirements surrounding assessment. Some will require you to send them a sample of work by a given deadline, others may send out someone to your centre to verify your work. In addition the requirements will vary depending upon the number of candidates that you have studying for the qualification. Most centres will have a designated person, normally the exams officer, who will receive the information regarding the requirements from the awarding body. Some tips to enable you to create effective quality processes within your institution are given below:

● Ensure that the candidate signs to confirm that it is their own work and has not been taken from any unacknowledged source. Any taped or videoed work has the candidate's name and entry number clearly identified. You may find this easier to do by asking the candidates to state their name and candidate number at the beginning of each tape/video section and providing a typed 'running order' for any external scrutiny.

● The marking tutor signs to confirm that the work seen has been verified as being from the candidate in question and that they have completed it without any outside assistance. If the marking tutor believes that extra support has been given to the candidate they must ensure that the help given is acceptable under the awarding body's guidelines. In these cases the marks given are normally for the proportion of the work that was

→

---

completed unaided. Again you should check with your awarding body for exact information.

- The internal verifier re-marks a set number of scripts and signs to confirm that they agree with all marks awarded.

- Any students who are statemented and may be using amanuensis are identified clearly for both internal and any external records.

- If, as the marking tutor or internal verifier, you are unable to sign that a particular piece of work belongs to a particular student it is unlikely that your awarding body will accept the work as part of the qualification's assessment.

These records should be kept centrally in case they are requested by the awarding body at any stage in the process.

Principles of assessment

Although I do not intend to go into great depth on the principles of assessment, as there are many books specialising in assessment that you could refer to – Gravells (2009), Tummons (2007) – it is important to note that there are several principles you need to be aware of when assessing your students.

Equity

As practitioners and human beings we can sometimes be subjective in our judgements and this can sometimes creep over into our assessment practices. However, as professionals, we are duty bound to ensure that we are fair and equitable in our assessments and that all learners are treated equally when we make our judgements. Many universities have moved to a 'blind' marking system to remove any bias or subjectivity that may be perceived to exist between teachers and learners. Within your own organisation there will be guidelines on the assessment processes to which you are required to conform, such as blind marking, or percentage number of scripts/assignments that need to be moderated. I suggest you look at these guidelines and if you are unsure about any of them ask a fellow practitioner for guidance.

Validity

Validity is concerned with the extent to which the assessment matches or links to the requirements of the awarding body and the extent to which we are measuring what we say we are. A learner should not be penalised for spelling and grammar if the assessment was not designed to test that element of their knowledge. Here we have a dilemma – do we mark or comment on grammatical and spelling issues if the assessment itself isn't concerned with them? In my own assessment I would normally mark an error to help the student in future work, and make a comment in the margin as to the correct spelling or grammar. However, I would never use these errors as a basis for judgement and would not feature them in the written overall feedback with phrases such as 'To improve you need to consider your spelling' if it wasn't relevant to the overall task.

Authenticity

Authenticity in assessment can have two distinct meanings. First, is the assessment authentic, does it mirror the real world in which the student would be working? Second, is the work produced by the learner authentic? Is it their own? Or have they copied it from a third party or source? Plagiarism has been and continues to be one of the most common problems with written work over the last five to ten years. The rise of the internet and other associated e-technologies make it very difficult for us to determine whether a piece of work is authentic. My own organisation has a piece of software called 'Turn it in' which can identify work that could have been copied and the source that it may have come from. Does your organisation have anything similar?

Sufficiency

Given that the diploma is awarded by an external agency we need to ensure that the assessments we produce provide sufficient coverage and depth of coverage to provide the evidence that our learners have achieved the set standard.

Reliability

Within assessments reliability is closely linked to accuracy and consistency. To ensure reliability we need to include moderation and cross-marking within our assessment processes to ensure that each assessor is working to the same standards.

Transparency

Do your learners know what they need to do to succeed? If you have a transparent system in place learners will understand what is required of them and the assessment will be closely linked to the outcomes of the course. Within my own subject area one of my learners felt very cheated that her project on a European holiday destination was referred as she used Egypt as the destination of choice. While Egypt is not technically in Europe it does fall under Europe when it comes to insurance guidelines and it was this definition she had used. As the teacher I needed to make the guidelines more transparent to ensure that the learners only chose geographical Europe! This is particularly important when the assessments are the summative assessments or are the externally assessed assessments. With the previous example the student concerned was able to make amends for the final piece of work. However, had this been an externally assessed piece of work she could have ended up with few or no marks.

Modes and methods of assessment

Assessment for Learning (AfL) and the pedagogy that underpins it should inform all of the work we do in the classroom. It is based on the principle that learners will achieve and improve if they understand why they are learning and what the long-term goal of their learning is. It is also based on the principle that the learners should be able to identify where they are in relation to achieving their long-term goal and how they can further progress towards the final outcome.

The DCSF has recently published its Strategy for AfL, which underpins the Framework for Learning, national strategies for secondary schools supported with funding to develop and embed them in all schools. The new Frameworks website can be found at www.standards.dcsf.gov.uk/secondary/frameworks.

Why not try this?

Go to the DCSF website. How will this strategy impact upon you as a diploma teacher?

Formal and informal assessment

For you as the teacher the most common modes of assessment for learning will be *formal* and *informal* assessment. Formal assessment is used to measure and record the student's learning, whereas informal assessment is the ongoing monitoring of the student during the lesson, course or programme.

Formal assessment can be summative (at the end) or formative, used to make judgements on whether, and to what extent, learning has happened. Another way of looking at 'formative' and 'summative' is that summative is the assessment of learning and comes towards the end of the course, while formative is the assessment for learning. As a mode of assessment formative can be used as a way to undertake periodic assessments of the progress learners are making, as it identifies strengths and weaknesses in their learning. This can be then used to inform the learners' individual learning plans (see Chapter 5).

> ## Why not try this?
>
> Consider your students. What types of formal and informal assessment do you use?
>
> Are there any issues or problems with these methods?

Assessing the diploma

Now we have considered the modes of assessment let us look at some of the methods of assessment that you could use as a diploma teacher and the advantages and disadvantages of each method.

Diplomas are assessed through a mix of exams and moderated internal assessment to reflect the practical nature of the learning. The different elements of the diploma, that is functional skills, principal learning and the project, are all assessed separately and the results combined to award the final diploma. For the learner this is advantageous in that they get credit for each element they achieve, which can be 'banked' and used to gain the final qualification when all of the elements are achieved. It also allows a learner to move between organisations, as the credit gained in one school or college can be used as accreditation of prior learning (APL) should the learner move to a different part of the country. In some cases it may also be possible to move between qualifications; for example, a learner who has been studying engineering and has achieved his or her functional skills element could transfer to the diploma in construction and the built environment, taking the credits with them.

Projects

Given the practical nature of the diploma qualifications a project as a means of assessment is part of the very core of the qualification. The assessment within a project can take many different forms – it could be a portfolio, a presentation or a display to name but a few. Projects can work well as both individual and group activities and as an assessment method can encourage independent learning and collaborative learning skills, in short, skills that are sought by employers and universities.

> ## TOP TIP!
>
> *As the teacher you need to ensure that the projects are managed effectively and that you as the facilitator set clear guidelines and indeed clear deadlines for your learners.*

Exams

Exams are also central to the diplomas and as a teacher your role is to prepare the learner for the examination and to ensure that they are ready to undertake the assessment. For the learner an examination can be a fearful experience, especially if they have had exam failures in the past. It is therefore important to allow the learners as much opportunity as possible to undertake mock questions to allow them to practise technique and gain confidence in their knowledge. With the diplomas the exams are externally set, so as the teacher you will not have to worry about extra marking. However, be aware that the exam results will be used to provide the benchmark statistics against which you could be measured.

Reports

Reports as a means of assessment are useful in the diploma as they can be linked to the real world and the learners can focus on a particular area to demonstrate their underpinning knowledge and the application of that knowledge in practice. For example, a learner on the construction diploma might be asked to write a health and safety report for a company following a field trip to a construction site. This would allow them to demonstrate their knowledge of health and safety legislation and also apply it to their experiences on the visit.

Displays and exhibitions

Within the diploma using displays and exhibitions as a means of assessment can range from a small-scale, in-house event to a full-blown exhibition that invites external guests. Consider the hair and beauty diploma: learners could stage a hair show, showcasing latest designs and fashion to a local community group; or learners on the media diploma could put on a fashion show for a local clothing company. This type of assessment can be extremely motivating for the learner and can also develop other skills, such as teamwork, functional maths (costing the room hire) and communication (publicity and sales).

TOP TIP!

Displays and exhibitions can be costly to support, so why not give the learners the added motivation of raising money for a local charity to encourage them to be more efficient with their spending.

Role play

Role play has its place in diploma assessments, in that it allows the learner to demonstrate a skill they may not be able to do in the workplace itself. For example, within the travel diploma a role-play assessment could be the checking, costing and booking of a holiday for a family of four (played by peers or other teachers). While this may be something that the learner would do in the workplace it is something that you may not get the opportunity to observe and therefore a simulation through role play provides an effective vehicle for the learner to demonstrate his or her skills.

Case study

Case studies can be used in a variety of ways to assess a learner. As a tool a case study can provide the learner with a range of information about a workplace, activity or specific organisation. The case study can then be used to assess how the learner uses his or her underpinning knowledge to answer a range of questions, create reports, deliver presentations, etc. Within the society, health and development diploma learners could be provided with a case study on obesity and eating habits and required to produce a display on cause and effect.

Portfolio

A portfolio is a collection of materials that are drawn together to provide the evidence that the learner has achieved a certain standard. As an assessment tool a portfolio can allow the learner to demonstrate their development in a particular subject over a period of time, or it can just be a collection of material linked to the learning outcomes of the qualification. Portfolio assessment is still very common in NVQ qualifications. However, critics of the portfolio believe it is just box ticking to demonstrate achievement and holds no real value in terms of learner development and distance travelled.

Why not try this?

Make a list of all the assessment methods that you use or have used. What are the advantages and disadvantages for the diploma learner?

Grading the diploma

Most awarding bodies will offer support and training to organisations on the assessment process and the grading of the diploma qualification.

The grading of the diploma will be reported in the following way:

- Foundation diploma: A*, A, B or ungraded (U).

- Higher diploma: A*, A, B, C or ungraded (U).

- Advanced diploma: A*, A, B, C, D, E or ungraded (U).

To be awarded a full diploma the learner will need to complete all of the elements including Functional skills and Additional and specialist learning. However, Principal learning, Functional skills and the project are also graded as separate and individual qualifications. The final diploma grade is derived from the aggregate score of Principal learning and the project. The next section will look at the different elements of the diploma and how it could be assessed and graded.

Principal learning

Each unit within the Principal learning is assessed and graded separately. The unit assessments are a combination of both internally and externally graded work. You will need to look at your particular specification to identify which units are internally assessed and which externally. For the internally assessed units each awarding body provides a format of the assessment for each unit within the diploma qualification specification, although you will have some freedom to tailor your assessment to what is available in your local area.

Within the diploma and the Principal learning component, one of the key areas that you will need to take into account is the assessment of the Personal, Learning and Thinking Skills (PLTS):

- independent enquiry;

- creative thinking;

- reflective learning;

- teamworking;

- self-management;

- effective participation.

All of these skills have been integrated into the requirements of each of the units of the qualification and as a teacher you will need to ensure that you identify where the learner has achieved these elements.

Generic learning

Functional skills

Functional skills (English, Mathematics and ICT) are components of Generic learning within the diploma that need to be assessed. At present Functional skills are assessed in different ways by different awarding bodies for the purposes of piloting a range of assessment approaches. Final decisions on the assessment of Functional skills are expected to be made in 2010.

Project

Learners will have to choose a topic to study; complete a log to document the progress of their project; plan, research and carry out their project and prepare a presentation on the outcome. Learners' performance in each of these stages will be marked by the teachers within the organisation to produce an overall project grade. You will also be able to identify the PLTS in this unit.

Work experience

Work experience itself is not assessed or graded, although you may be able to use it as a case study for some of your other assessments. You will need to record that the learner has completed the work experience element of the diploma.

Additional specialist learning (ASL)

As each learner is unique the grading of the ASL that they choose will follow the guidelines of that particular qualification.

The diploma assessor

As the diplomas grow in popularity and more institutions start to offer them as an alternative qualification two new types of assessor role have been identified that are specific to the diploma: lead assessor and domain assessor.

A lead assessor will be appointed if a consortium plans to offer a range of diploma lines. This person will have the overall responsibility for the internal assessment and internal assessment policies for all the lines being offered. They will also be responsible for the administrative requirements of the diploma.

A domain assessor is the assessor responsible for each of the lines of learning being offered, and if the organisation offers only one line of learning takes on the duties of the lead assessor. However, if the organisation offers more than one line of learning the domain assessor reports to and is responsible to the lead assessor.

UsefulWebsite

For more information on these two roles, visit the website http://testsandexams.qcda.gov.uk/libraryAssets/media/19722_DIPLOMAS_ToPrint.pdf for the publication, 'A training guide for lead and domain assessors'.

Recording assessment – the diploma way?

Record keeping can feel like a major chore in the day-to-day activities of a teacher. However, it is crucial that you keep and maintain records of your learners. What records should you be keeping? You will need to know how well each learner is progressing with the units and the outcomes within each unit as a bare minimum, as this may form the basis of tutorials and learning plan discussions. I would also suggest that you keep a record of the progress of the entire group. That way you can identify if any learners are falling behind, or whether any of the units may be proving difficult for the entire group.

TOP TIP!

A simple grid can be used for both sets of records and if kept electronically can be easily updated. Other records you may wish to keep are those of tutorial discussions.

Reflecting on practice

Jen is responsible for the Advanced Diploma in Creative and Media at a local sixth form college. She has recently requested that the team revisit the documentation they are using to record the students and the students' progress. She receives the following record/tracking sheets as examples of the documentation in use:

Name	UNIT – grade						
	1	2 (External)	3 (External)	4	5	6	Comments
Peter							
Josh							
Andy							
Mark							

(N/S non-submission)

Name	UNIT 4								
	Outcome 1		Outcome 2			Outcome 3			Comments
Assessment criteria	A	B	A	B	C	A	B	C	
Peter									
Josh									
Andy									
Mark									

Consider the following:

What information could these two pieces of documentation provide and what other information would you benefit from as a tutor?

E-assessment

This chapter on assessment would not be complete without reference to e-assessment and e-portfolios. One of the key strategic objectives of the Qualifications and Curriculum Authority (QCA) was that by 2009:

- all new qualifications would have an option of on-screen assessment;
- awarding bodies would accept e-portfolios;
- assessment on demand would start to be introduced by awarding bodies.

Where does e-assessment figure in your diploma? How could you use it more effectively?

The Chartered Institute of Educational Assessors

Assessment as part of a teaching role, or as a role within its own right, has its own professional body. The Chartered Institute of Educational Assessors (CIEA) is 'dedicated to supporting the needs of everyone involved in educational assessment. We exist to provide support, recognition and professional representation for the assessment community' (www.ciea.org.uk, accessed 12 March 2009).

As a professional organisation the membership is made up of a variety of people involved in the assessment process, including moderators and first markers, who work across a range of educational establishments, such as secondary schools, colleges, universities and training centres.

The organisation also provides training and additional qualifications in assessment that may be of interest for your own professional development.

> **UsefulWebsite**
>
> Visit the Chartered Institute of Educational Assessors website and see what support is available to you.
>
> www.ciea.org.uk

Conclusion

This chapter has explored some of the principles and concepts of assessment, and while not exhaustive in its discussion has provided some models of assessment that you may wish to use when teaching the diploma, together with examples of documentation which could be adapted for your use. An overview of the diploma grading and the assessor types has been provided, plus linkages to further qualifications that you may wish to consider when engaged in diploma delivery.

> **Key ideas summary**
>
> - What are your reasons for assessing?
> - Who determines the assessment methods?
> - What is the assessment process?
> - What types of recording documentation will be the most beneficial to you?
> - What additional qualifications could you study for as a diploma assessor?

Going further

Gravells, A. (2009) *Principles and Practice of Assessment in the Lifelong Learning Sector*, Exeter: Learning Matters.

Haywood, L.E. (2007) 'Curriculum, pedagogies and assessment in Scotland: The quest for social justice. "Ah Kent yir faither"', *Assessment in Education: Principles, Policy and Practice*, 14, 2, 251–68.

Scales, P. (2008) *Teaching in the Lifelong Learning Sector*, Maidenhead: Open University Press.

Tummons, J. (2007) *Assessing Learning in the Lifelong Learning Sector*, Exeter: Learning Matters.

www.aqa.org.uk

www.ciea.org.uk

www.qcda.gov.uk

www.standards.dcsf.gov.uk/secondary/frameworks

http://testsandexams.qcda.gov.uk/libraryAssets/media/19722_DIPLOMAS_To Print.pdf

Functional skills and the diploma

What this chapter will explore:

- Defining functional skills
- Why functional skills?
- Functional/key/basic skills
- Functional Skills Standards
- Identification of functional skills activities
- Assessing functional skills
- Tips for successful implementation

This chapter will explore functional skills, and their place within the diploma lines. It will examine the different methods of teaching functional skills to 14–19-year-old learners, together with case studies and activities for you to consider in your own setting.

'Functional skills are vital to the personal development of all learners aged 14 and above.'

(Qualifications and Curriculum Authority, 2007, p 3)

Defining functional skills

Before we can really start to examine functional skills in any detail and make choices regarding their delivery within the diploma, we really need to understand what functional skills are and why they have been developed.

Functional skills are practical skills in English, mathematics (maths) and information and communication technology (ICT). They are defined as the skills that 'enable everyone to work confidently, effectively and independently in life and at work' (www.aqa.org, accessed 26 March 2009). As a qualification they have been piloted in the UK since 2007 and the first national teaching is due to start September 2010. As part of their development the government originally envisaged that by 2012 all young people would need to achieve their functional skills at Level 2 in order to be awarded a GCSE at grade C or above in the subject. However, a recent decision by the government has seen this vision dropped as OfQual investigations concluded that a 'basic skills hurdle that was separate from the main GCSE would cause problems with the perceived fairness of the outcomes as well as technical difficulties. This would be unacceptable and risk bringing the qualifications into disrepute' (BBC, 2009).

Why functional skills?

So where have functional skills come from and how are they different from key skills and basic skills? Functional skills have been developed following the 14–19 Education and Skills White Paper (DCSF, February 2005), the Skills White Paper (DCSF, March 2005), and in response to employment needs and employer requests to provide a workforce that is competent and able to compete in an ever-increasing competitive environment. Functional skills will be available at entry Levels 1–3, Levels 1 and 2, and they will exist as a stand-alone qualification, in addition to being an integral element of the diploma. Functional skills will eventually replace key skills at Levels 1 and 2.

So how are they different to key skills, basic skills, skills for life and core skills?

To answer that question we will first have to look at the other skills.

Key skills

Key skills are defined as 'essential, generic skills which are the basis of all successful lifelong learning and development' (Scales, 2008, p 253). Six key skills exist at the time of writing:

1. Communication.

2. Application of number.

3. Information technology.

4. Improving own learning and performance.

5. Working with others.

6. Problem-solving.

Each of the skills are available at Levels 1–4. In order to achieve a key skills qualification the learner must produce a portfolio of evidence and, for the first three, communication, application of number and ICT, also pass an externally assessed test. Key skills were initially established following the Dearing Review of post-16 education (Dearing, 1996) and replaced what was previously known as core or common skills.

Basic skills

Basic skills are defined as, 'the ability to read, write and speak in English/Welsh and to use mathematics at a level necessary to progress at work and in society in general' (Basic Skills Agency: www.archive.basic-skills.co.uk). Basic skills as a concept arose from the publishing of the government report '*A Fresh Start*' (Moser, 1999), more commonly known as the Moser Report. This report suggested that at least 7 million adults had literacy and numeracy levels at or below those expected of 11 year olds. Following this report the government launched the Skills for Life strategy, which included standards for literacy and numeracy programmes with five levels being available, entry Levels 1–3, Level 1 (foundation) and Level 2 (intermediate).

Skills for life

The term skills for life tends to be used synonymously with basic skills, and are the skills referred to by the Skills Strategy as being the skills needed to up-skill our workforce. Skills for life tend to be aimed at the adult learner, whereas the key skills framework tends to be aimed at the 14–19-year-old market.

As previously mentioned functional skills will replace key skills Levels 1 and 2 in communication, ICT and application of number, the other key skills look set to remain at present, as do the skills for life in literacy, numeracy, ICT and English language (ESOL).

Core or common skills

The term common skills can have several different meanings; in some cases common skills are the same as key skills, particularly in Scottish education. In other areas common skills and the common skills framework are used to describe the underpinning skills that a teacher working in the lifelong learning sector would need, commonly referred to as the *minimum core*, and covering literacy, numeracy and ICT. Further references to core skills can be found within the '*The Common Core of Skills and Knowledge for the Children's Workforce*' – often referred to as 'The Common Core' (DfES, 2005). This reference to core skills sets out the basic skills and knowledge needed by people whose work (paid or voluntary) brings them into regular contact with children, young people and families. Again the skills and knowledge area within this use of the term have been divided into six:

1. Effective communication and engagement with children, young people and families.
2. Child and young person development.
3. Safeguarding and promoting the welfare of the child.
4. Supporting transitions.
5. Multi-agency working.
6. Sharing information.

Why not try this?

To find out more about the common core affecting either a teacher in the lifelong learning sector or someone working with children, young people and families go to the following websites: www.everychildmatters.gov.uk and www.lluk.org.

Teaching and learning in functional skills

At the time of writing teachers qualified to teach both basic and key skills will be able to teach functional skills. So what does this mean for us as teachers?

Functional skills are the skills that allow the learner to solve problems and therefore any activities we provide should allow the learner to make their own decisions and choices. One of the key decisions that your organisation will need to make is whether they treat functional skills as a separate element, delivered within the English, maths and ICT classes, or whether it should be delivered as part of the applied learning within the diploma. It is my belief that as teachers we should be embedding functional skills into the curriculum rather than allowing them to be stand-alone and taught as separate entities. In other words, making use of naturally occurring activities within the teaching of the subject to help the learner develop the skills. The diploma as a qualification has both workplace and work-related learning and therefore is an ideal vehicle to provide these naturally occurring activities. So how do we as teachers make use of these types of activities to encourage the development of functional skills, and what types of activities can we use within our applied learning classrooms?

To start with we need to be able to develop and build our learners' skills so that they feel comfortable in applying those skills to practical situations. A range of learning and teaching strategies are available to you to build skills and, although not exhaustive, the following gives you a brief overview of what you can use.

Demonstration

Many teachers believe that learners cannot acquire a skill unless they have been taught that skill (QCDA, 2008). Demonstration as a tool allows you to involve the learners in the process while providing them with the opportunity to practise the skill being taught. Look back at Chapter 2, on learning and teaching. Demonstration as a strategy allows you to make full use of Kolb's learning cycle through observation, practical application, reflection and reapplication. As a strategy for skills building it can help the learner understand the underpinning principles surrounding a particular concept and if used as a group activity can provide more opportunities for developing the more and broader skills of working with others and problem solving.

Explanation

As a strategy explanation allows the learner to build upon ideas and make connections to other information. Again, if we use the concept map discussed in Chapter 2 as an example, we can see how a learner may be able to generate ideas that allow them to better understand abstract ideas and make judgements on similarities or differences.

Group work

Group work allows the learners to practise their skills with each other and learn from each other. If used effectively it again can be linked into the wider key skills.

Relating this to your own subject area and context

Consider one of your learners working in the construction trade. Would you want him/her to build your new conservatory if they were unable to calculate area and the materials needed to complete the job successfully? Another example – would you want to eat in a restaurant where the staff were unable to give you the correct change or even heat your meal to the correct temperature?

As a teacher there will be many naturally occurring activities to allow you to develop and embed functional skills, regardless of your subject and line of learning area. Indeed research suggests that the embedding of skills encourages a more positive attitude to literacy, maths and ICT and in addition improves the actual achievement rates (Casey et al., 2006).

Functional Skills Standards

Functional Skills Standards were developed by the Qualifications and Curriculum Authority and first published in 2007 as the draft standards to be used within the pilot of functional skills (QCA, 2007). The standards explain the difference between the different qualification levels and identify the key factors that will allow you to determine the learners' proficiency in that particular skill. Proficiency is assessed on:

- the complexity of situations and activities;
- the technical demand associated with these activities;
- a learner's level of familiarity with the task or activity;
- the level of independence a learner can use to complete the activity.

Each level identifies a skill standard and a range of activities that may be used to demonstrate coverage of the standards. This element of the standards, coverage and range are not prescriptive, but only indicative. The functional skill level is determined by the learner's ability to use and apply this information for 'real-life' situations.

At the time of writing the functional skills standards included the following (the table is adapted from www.qca.org.uk):

Functional English	Speaking and listening Reading Writing
Functional maths	Process skills Choose an approach to tackle the problem, formulate a model using mathematics, use mathematics to provide answers, interpret and check the results, evaluate the model and approach, explain the analysis and results, apply and adapt this experience in other situations as they arise.
Functional ICT	Use ICT systems Find and select information Develop, present and communicate information

Why not try this?

Go to the QCA website and download the latest version of the Functional Skills Standards. Have there been many changes since the pilot version? If so, why do you think this is?

Possible activities for functional skills learning and teaching

English

Functional English skills are arguably the easiest skills to embed in our everyday teaching. As teachers we regularly ask our learners to produce written accounts, make presentations on a given topic, and gather information from a range of sources. It is therefore a relatively simple task to apply the standards to the work we ask our students to complete. For example, if we take the diploma in hospitality we could set a piece of classwork that requires the learners to gather information on a range of diets and dietary requirements. Once they have the relevant information we could ask them to design a menu suitable for a diner with coeliac disease (allergic to gluten). This allows them to select relevant information from the range they have gathered. Following the completion of the menu the learner could then explain, with justification, his or her menu choice to the group.

Other examples of activities that you could consider include:

● Completion of forms as part of a customer enquiry (role play).

● Completion of application forms as part of a work-related lesson.

- Respond to information provided over the telephone, e.g. taking a table booking at a restaurant, dealing with a customer complaint.

- Present an idea for a group event (beauty, business).

- Produce a leaflet or flyer for the company in which they complete the work experience.

- Interview members of staff/students about healthy eating (hospitality).

Why not try this?

Create a learning activity at Level 2 that covers the three main areas of the functional English skills for your subject area.

How could you adapt this activity to cater for a Level 1 student?

Maths

Maths occurs in every part of everyday life, so again it should be relatively simple to embed functional maths into your teaching without the students realising that they are actually doing maths! Let's take Unit 6 of the Level 2 Diploma in Creative and Media – Creative Teamwork. As part of this unit the learner becomes involved in the planning and development of an event, which includes the production of a schedule or action plan for the event itself. As part of this the students could produce a cost plan for the implementation of the event, produce a schematic diagram that shows the layout for the event, with appropriate measurements and 3-D drawings, produce break-even charts for ticket sales, and countless other numeracy-based activities.

Other examples of activities that you could consider include:

- Read bus or rail timetables.

- Draw schematic diagrams.

- Create 3-D images.

- Measure out ingredients.

- Create a simple costing plan for an event or activity.

- Create graphs or pie charts comparing temperature or hours of sunshine.

Why not try this?

Create a learning activity at Level 1 that covers the functional maths skills for your subject area.

How could you adapt this activity to cater for a Level 2 student?

ICT

Many of our learners will be digital natives – that is, familiar with ICT – more than we as teachers are at times. As a functional skill ICT shouldn't be seen in isolation. If our learners are gathering information for a project, why not ask them to do it via the internet; if they are producing cost plans, make use of Excel or other spreadsheet software. If they are working on group activities and tasks why not set up 'group emails' and 'wikis' for the purpose of the activity.

Other examples of activities that you could consider include:

● Creation of simple forms to store data.

● Enter data into documents and edit.

● Use 'pod casts' to record group meetings.

● Produce a short promotional film or video for an organisation within the subject area.

Why not try this?

Create a learning activity at Level 2 that covers the functional ICT skills for your subject area.

Reflecting on practice

Embedding functional skills at Heanor Gate Science College

Heanor Gate Science College is an 11–18 school, working within a local diploma consortium, Ripley and Heanor Learning Community. They have partnered with a local tourist attraction to create resources that help fulfil the requirements of functional skills in English, maths and ICT. One resource is a functional skills trail that requires students to answer a series of

→

questions, and gather information on the tourist attraction. Groups of young people visit the attraction and are provided with a work booklet that provides them with information they need to complete the trail together with spaces for their answers.

The teacher responsible for the development of the resource works on the IT diploma and has added an additional task specifically for her learners, which requires them to produce a presentation suitable to be sent to schools for school visits or to be displayed in local tourist information centres.

The resource has been piloted across the schools in the local consortium and has proved to be a success with the learners.

Consider the following:

1. What local attractions could you work with to develop similar materials?
2. What advantages and disadvantages might there be to embedding the skills in this manner?

Other methods of functional skill delivery

While the previous section dealt with the embedding of functional skills into the principal learning of the diploma, it must be noted here that at present the assessment for functional skills is not contextualised to the subject area of the diploma and the learners will need to demonstrate that they can apply their learning to other areas in the assessment.

As mentioned earlier in the chapter your organisation will need to take the decision on how to deliver functional skills, and this section highlights some of the other delivery approaches you may wish to consider.

Discrete

In this approach the functional skills are delivered entirely by specialists and delivered separately from the diploma.

Partly embedded

Here the functional skills are still taught by specialists but are applied across a range of diploma lines.

Mostly embedded

Here the skills are taught by specialists but are reinforced and applied in context across the diploma lines.

Fully embedded

Taught by teachers across the diploma through naturally occurring opportunities within the context of the principal learning.

Reflecting on practice

Discrete delivery

College X delivers functional skills to its learners on a discrete basis. Each learner has two hours taught classes for each functional skill per week. In the classes the learners are given a problem to solve. Each learner must then produce a plan of how they intend to solve the problem, complete the plan, check the findings and produce a report on the findings together with an evaluation of the process. The college believes that delivery in this way enables the learners to master the skills and transfer the mastery to any context.

Consider the following:

1. What are the advantages and disadvantages of this method for your organisation?

2. How do you think the learners will react to two hours of 'maths, English, ICT'?

Assessing functional skills

The assessment process for functional skills has been developed by the QCA and ensures that the awarding bodies responsible for functional skills assessment take into account the application of the skill in a real-life context. Assessments can be either task or test based, or a mixture of the two, and each awarding body has created its own design and marking schemes. The only proviso that the QCA has made regarding the design of assessment is that each element of the skill must be addressed, that is, speaking and listening, reading and writing for the English tests.

Why not try this?

Go to your awarding body's website and have a look at the assessment examples they provide.

Currently, awarding bodies offer assessment opportunities for the functional skills twice a year. Teachers and organisations can choose to enter the learner for assessment when they judge them to be ready at any time throughout the duration of the diploma qualification, or alternatively can enter them at the end of the programme. My approach has been to enter learners halfway through their programme. This allows both the teachers and the learners to further identify any areas of weakness should the learner not succeed. Thus, ensuring that additional support and/or practice is provided in those areas allows the learner maximum opportunity to succeed on the second attempt.

TOP TIP!

Here are some tips for the successful implementation of functional skills.

The first year of the functional skills pilot identified several areas that institutions should be aware of to ensure that the functional skills element of the diploma is introduced successfully. Some of these tips have been reproduced here in full from the DCSF's National Strategies website at www.standards.dcsf.gov.uk/nationalstrategies (last accessed 27/03/09).

Work collaboratively

Learners in diploma consortia may well access different components of the diploma framework in different centres. It is crucial therefore for centres and consortia to decide where the functional skills will be taught and how, through collaborative dialogue and planning, those skills will be developed and transferred into other contexts.

Consider the three-stage process of skills development

When revising schemes of work ready for delivery it may be useful to focus on where you will provide opportunities for learners to build functional skills, to develop and apply them to a range of purposeful contexts and to demonstrate that learners have secured or 'mastered' those skills.

Review and revise

This means reviewing and revising what you currently do, not redesigning the scheme of work from scratch.

Evaluate progress critically

It is important to evaluate progress critically to identify not only what needs to be improved but also what has gone well and why, and to build on those experiences in order to inform future developments.

Reflecting on practice

The travel and tourism course tutor has produced an integrated assignment that allows the learner to demonstrate his/her competency with functional skills.

The assignment is split into several different tasks set within a travel agency.

The main part of the assessment is a role play in which the learner has to meet with a client and help them to choose an appropriate holiday for a family of four, two adults and two children between 5 and 11 years of age.

The learner is provided with the basic requirements of the family, in terms of holiday duration, dates, type of accommodation, number of rooms and the facilities they require.

It is the role of the learner to identify an appropriate destination and hotel, provide a holiday costing for the family and explain the choice to them. The explanation involves showing the family where the resort is on the map and explaining why this choice meets their requirements. At the end of the role play the learner is required to complete a record sheet for the enquiry and store the details for future reference.

Consider the following:

1. Using the Functional Skills Standards identify which of the functional skills elements are being addressed.

2. What additional activities could be added to this scenario to expand the functional skills that are being addressed?

Conclusion

Functional skills have been developed in the three key areas of English, maths and ICT and will be an integral part of the diploma, forming part of the mandatory element that learners will need to achieve. There are several different ways in which functional skills can be delivered within the classroom and as a teacher you need to ensure that your delivery best meets the needs of the learner and the organisation within which you teach.

Key ideas summary

- Functional skills are the key elements of English, maths and ICT that allow a learner to work independently, confidently and effectively – discuss.

- How do functional skills differ from basic and key skills?

- How can you as the teacher embed functional skills effectively into your programmes?

- Within a consortium, who should be responsible for ensuring that functional skills are developed?

Going further

BBC (2009) 'GCSE basic skills pledge scrapped', *BBC News*, 2 April; at http://news.bbc.co.uk/1/low/education/7979267.stm

Casey, H., Cara, O., Eldred, J., Grief, S., Hodge, R., Ivanicv, R., Jupp, T., Lopez, D. and McNeil, B. (2006) 'You wouldn't expect a maths teacher to teach plastering', in *Embedding Literacy, Language and Numeracy on post-16 vocational programmes: The Impact on Learning and Achievement*, London: NRDC.

DCSF (February 2005) 14–19 Education and Skills White Paper, Norwich: HMSO; at www.dcsf.gov.uk/14–19/documents/14-19whitepaper.pdf

DCSF (March 2005) Skills White Paper: 'Getting on in work', at www.dcsf.gov.uk/publications/skillsgettingon

Dearing, R. (1996) *Review of Qualifications for 16–19 year olds*, London: Schools Curriculum and Assessment Authority.

DfES (2005) *The Common Core of Skills and Knowledge for the Children's Workforce,* (Every Child Matters change for children), London: DfES; at www.everychildmatters.gov.uk

Leitch, S (2006) *Prosperity for All in a Global Economy: World-class Skills*, London: HMSO.

Moser, Sir Claus (chair) (1999) *Improving Literacy and Numeracy; A Fresh Start*, Report of the Working Group, London: DfEE.

QCA (2007) *Functional Skills; Essential Skills for Work and Life*, London: QCA; at www.qca.org.uk/functionalskills

QCDA (2008) *Guidance and Illustrations: Functional Skills Delivery and the Diploma*, London: QCDA.

Scales, P. (2008) *Teaching in the Lifelong learning Sector*, Maidenhead: Open University Press.

www.aqa.org

www.archive.basic-skills.co.uk

www.dfes.gov.uk/keyskills

www.dfes.gov.uk/readwriteplus

www.everychildmatters.gov.uk

www.lluk.org

www.lsneducation.org/functionalskills – Functional Skills Support programme

www.standards.dscf.gov.uk/nationalstrategies

www.totallyskilled.co.uk

Information, advice and guidance, and individual learning plans

What this chapter will explore:

- The definition of information, advice and guidance (IAG)
- IAG Standards
- The definition of individual learning plans (ILPs)
- The reasons for IAG/ILP within the diploma
- Personalised learning and the ILP

Information, advice and guidance, as its name would imply, refers to the help that is provided to our young learners to aid them in making appropriate choices regarding their career aspirations. This chapter will explore the origins of the concept of IAG and examine some of the ways in which IAG could work within the diploma qualification.

'"Information, advice and guidance" is a key element of Local Authority integrated youth support services. It is an umbrella term. It covers a range of activities and interventions that help young people to become more self-reliant and better able to manage their personal and career development, including learning.'

(DCSF, 2008)

The definition of IAG

From April 2008 the responsibility for information, advice and guidance was removed from the Connexions partnerships and devolved to local authorities. As a result of this change a set of 12 guiding principles were developed to ensure that young people were provided with consistently high and impartial advice and guidance regarding their learning and work choices. AG is an integral part of the 14–19 framework and the diploma lines and we as teachers need to be aware of the IAG Standards and their implications for us and our learners. As a key part of the diploma the IAG includes the following:

- provision of accurate and impartial information about learning and career opportunities;
- provision of information on progression;
- provision of specialist support to help young people develop new perspectives and make progress towards their individual goals.

It is also directly linked to the *Every Child Matters* (ECM) agenda and as a concept helps to contribute to the achievement of the five outcomes: be healthy, be safe, enjoy and achieve, make a positive contribution and achieve economic well-being.

IAG Standards

The table opposite (DCSF, 2008) summarises the 12 IAG Standards and gives a brief overview of how the standards could be implemented.

Standard	Implementation
Young people are informed about how information, advice and guidance services can help them and how to access the services they need	Provision of impartial advice and signposting to the appropriate advice. Use of different advice and guidance services within the education setting, e.g. Connexions
Young people receive the information, advice and guidance on personal well-being and financial capability issues that they need	Confidentiality assured. Referral to specialist services where appropriate
Young people have the information they need to make well-informed and realistic decisions about learning and career options	Provision of information on a full range of careers, progression routes, the labour market, pay, university courses and fees
Young people have the advice and guidance that they need to make well-informed and realistic decisions about learning and careers	Accessible and timely provision. Impartiality
Information, advice and guidance services promote equality of opportunity, celebrate diversity and challenge stereotypes	Accessibility and equity for all
Young people (reflecting the make-up of their communities) are engaged in the design, delivery and evaluation of information, advice and guidance provision	Peer support groups, peer mentoring and advice
Parents and carers know how information, advice and guidance services can help their children and know how these services are accessed	Parents made aware of the range of advice givers
Information, advice and guidance providers understand their roles and responsibilities	Collaborative working
Programmes of career and personal development for young people are planned and provided collaboratively	Collaborative working
Staff providing information, advice and guidance are appropriately qualified, work to relevant professional standards and receive continuing professional development (CPD)	CPD and staffing need audits
Information, advice and guidance services are regularly and systematically monitored, reviewed and evaluated, and actions are taken to improve services in response to the findings	Feedback mechanism in place
Processes for commissioning impartial information, advice and guidance services are effective and result in services that meet the needs of parents/carers and young people	Arrangements made to ensure that all provision is meeting the needs of the young person

Responsibility for the standards falls to local authorities, learning providers and external information, advice and guidance providers working together collaboratively under the leadership of the local authority.

Why not try this?

Using the 12 standards from the table on page 71, identify which areas you feel would be part of your role as a 14–19 teacher.

What types of IAG do you feel you would need to provide?

How could you ensure that you provided the correct information, guidance and advice to your learners?

Create a database of other people that you would be working with on information, advice and guidance.

NB You may need to consider the Data Protection Act here.

TOP TIP!

Remember IAG is a collaborative process involving multiple agencies, e.g. Connexions, the local authority, schools and colleges. You will not be expected to be the sole adviser for your students. However, you should be prepared to provide information on career progression and progression to higher education as part of your role as a diploma teacher, after all you are the 'subject' expert in the eyes of your learners.

It is important to note here that IAG is part of a larger governmental remit that includes career education guidance (CEG), and many documents refer to the two elements together, as career education, information, advice and guidance (CEIAG).

'In a complex and changing world all young people need access to good quality, comprehensive and impartial information, advice and guidance (IAG). They also need good quality careers education in schools.'

(DCSF, 2007)

CEIAG includes all of the standards that are related to IAG but in addition it includes the following (adapted from Connexions):

- Careers education – a planned programme of group activities in the curriculum that give students knowledge and skills for planning and managing their careers.

- Careers information – the provision of accurate, up-to-date printed and electronic resources on opportunities, progression routes, choices and occupations, including where to find help and how to access it.

- Work-related learning – experiences within and outside the curriculum that help young people to learn 'about, through, and for' the world of work.

- Personalised support and guidance – help for individuals to manage their learning and progression to the next stage.

- Careers guidance – help from specialist advisers to encourage individual learners to identify long-term goals and plan steps to attain them.

As a concept CEIAG could play a key role in helping you and your 14–19 learners by providing the following support to your diploma delivery:

- helping all learners develop work-related skills;

- demonstrating links between living, learning and earning;

- challenging preconceptions and stereotypes;

- increasing motivation and promoting a positive attitude towards learning;

- building self-confidence, self-reliance and raising ambitions;

- improving progression by raising awareness of all the opportunities available in learning and work;

- reducing drop-out rates and opening new doorways.

Why not try this?

In what way could you incorporate CEIAG into your curriculum?

Consider ways in which you could embed some of the elements listed above into your teaching.

Make a list of all the contacts you could use either within your workplace or from outside of the workplace who could support the CEIAG.

Potential issues with IAG

One of the key concerns regarding IAG was raised by Ofsted in an initial evaluation of the 14–19 implementation process. This concern was linked to the impartiality of advice given to learners aged 16. This is further supported by research undertaken by Connexions, which considers bias within IAG. Other potential problems that you may come across with IAG is the point in time at which IAG is carried out, (that is, is it early enough for the learners to make informed choices?) and also how up to date the information is that you are providing.

> ### Why not try this?
>
> What types of continuing professional development (CPD) might you need to undertake to ensure that the advice you were providing to your learners was impartial and up to date?

The definition of ILPs

What are ILPs and how do they fit with IAG and the diploma?

Individual learning plans (ILPs) were initially developed for Skills for Life learners to enable them to monitor progress towards their final goal. However, as one of the underpinning philosophies of the diploma qualification is the need for students to have a personalised learning experience and personal goals, ILPs have become an essential tool for diploma teachers, allowing us to manage our learners and their progress towards their individual goals. Essentially an ILP is produced as a result of initial and diagnostic assessment of the learner and is drawn up in negotiation with the learner to set their individual goals. The negotiation element of the ILP process is crucial in that it allows the learner to take control of their own learning, while at the same time allowing you as the teacher to challenge and stretch the learner's aspirations. As a tool the ILP has become an essential process in what is referred to as 'The Learning Journey' (DfES, 2004). This journey is summarised below:

1. Sign posting/referral.

2. Screening.

3. Initial assessment.

4. Diagnostic assessment.

5. ILP.

6. Summative assessment.

7. Formative assessment.

For the diploma the initial assessment element is used to assess the learner's skills and identify the appropriate level that the student should be placed at. It also identifies the programme that the learner should be placed upon. In diploma terms it forms part of and is intrinsically linked to information advice and guidance. For you as the 14–19 teacher the initial assessment could comprise of an evaluation of the learner's literacy, numeracy and ICT skills together with an analysis of the support needs that would have to be in place for the learner to succeed at the given level of diploma. This analysis may be simply a GCSE grade or you could include a short test to identify the level at which they are operating. In addition you may wish to include information on any medical conditions or learning difficulties that the learner may have, for example dyslexia, colour blindness or any illness that may impact upon the learning.

The diagnostic element of the learner's journey allows us as the teacher to identify the learner's strengths and weaknesses and any gaps in their skills or knowledge. This diagnostic assessment with the learner should identify their career aspirations and start to identify additional or specialist learning that will allow them to reach their goal. This is where your specialist subject knowledge will be beneficial, as you will be able to provide impartial advice on the areas that would give the learner the competitive advantage they may need for the labour market or university place.

However, as previously discussed there are other organisations that you can use or signpost your learners to for further advice. Additional information you may wish to gather at this stage could include any previous related learning that the learner may have completed. This information may provide evidence to credit the learner with some of the elements of their qualification through the accreditation of prior learning process as discussed in Chapter 3.

You may wish to record their expectations of the course and any issues they may have surrounding the qualification. For example, a learner may be worried about the reality of studying for a full diploma award and the additional and/or specialist learning that you have suggested. Once collected, all of this initial diagnostic information, together with the information from the initial assessment, is used to compile the learner's individual learning plan.

So what does a learning plan look like?

There are many different examples of ILPs, and a sample is included in Appendix 4. The ILP format is, to a certain extent, immaterial if it provides the relevant details that both the tutor and learner can use to monitor progress. As a minimum it should fulfil a number of basic functions:

- plan the student's programme;

- monitor the student's progress;

- keep a record of the student's achievement.

In addition it should set out the learner's goals, whether they are long-term career goals or short-term immediate goals, such as gain a Level 2 English qualification. They should also include timescales for each of the goals that can be monitored in tutorials, and a timetable for learning.

In conclusion an ILP is a 'route map' that highlights how students will achieve the qualification in question and so complete the 'learning journey'.

As a teacher you may find that some of your learners will have common goals and career aspirations which have led them to study the diploma. However, each learner will be unique in terms of their learning style, support needs, prior experiences and qualifications. One of the criticisms of the ILP as a learning tool is that it is quite often a generic document that does not take into account these differences, and as such it becomes a barrier to learning rather than a tool for learning as learners struggle to either meet the generic targets set for them or are not sufficiently challenged.

Advantages of ILPs

ILPs should be working documents that are regularly reviewed with the learner.

Discussion point – Who has 'ownership' of the ILP?

In considering the above you may wish to think about where the ILP is kept, and how easy it is for the learner to access it and make changes.

To the learner the ILP provides an illustration of the steps they need to take to achieve their career goals and aspirations. It allows them to remain on track and should, if used properly, motivate and encourage them in their learning journey. For you as the teacher it provides an overview of an individual's progress and enables you to monitor your learners more effectively. Furthermore, the ILP as a document is seen as being good practice by Ofsted and any inspection will examine the ILP and how it is used in practice.

'Inspectors will consider the extent to which teachers and trainers work with learners to develop individual learning plans that are informed by initial assessment and reviewed and updated regularly.'

(Ofsted, 2006, p 180)

Recent Ofsted inspections have identified three areas that demonstrate ILP strengths:

1. Effective use of individual learning plans.

2. Good individual learning plans.

3. Good development of individual learning plans.

In addition to this the Excellence Gateway (www.excellencegateway.org.uk) provides a series of questions that should be asked of the ILP pro forma. These are reproduced here in full:

● Does the pro forma you use have sections that reflect the requirements of all those involved in the delivery of training (employers, funding bodies, awarding bodies, assessors, tutors, specialist support staff)?

● List any amendments that are necessary.

● Take a sample of individual learning plans from across your provision. Is each plan individual to the learner, reflecting each learner's initial assessment (including necessary support and taking account of previous experience and qualifications) and goals (with dates for achieving various milestones such as individual units, key skills, etc.)?

● How have learners been involved in writing their individual learning plans and in updating them as required?

● How are targets broken down so that learners know the steps that they are expected to achieve and when they should do so (clear and measurable)?

● Is there any good practice that could be shared between programmes (if 'yes' list it)?

● How are individual learning plans used during review/tutorial activities?

● Do all those who require it have access to the individual learning plans?

● Are individual learning plans 'live' documents?

● How do quality systems check how well individual learning plans are being used?

Why not try this?

Take the ILP format that your establishment uses and answer the questions posed above.

Should the ILP be adapted in light of your responses? If so, how?

Personalised learning and the ILP

As we have already identified earlier in this chapter each one of your students is unique and therefore will have their own unique individual learning plan. The diploma philosophy is that each student will undertake a personalised learning programme to allow them to achieve their own goals and aspirations. This section will examine personalised learning and what it means for both you as the teacher and your learner.

What do we mean by personalised learning?

According to Miliband (2004) personalised learning means is about organising education around the needs, interests and aptitudes of each learner. For the teacher and the organisation this means that we need to ensure that our teaching is linked closely to the ways in which our learners learn and that through matching teaching to learner preference we are ensuring that everyone, regardless of their ability, can achieve. Look back at Chapter 2 for learning styles to remind yourself about the different learning preferences.

Gilbert (2007, p 7) defines personalised learning as:

> 'Taking a highly structured and responsive approach to each child's and young person's learning, in order that all are able to progress, achieve and participate.'

So the concept of personalised learning is the ability to shape and decide upon their own curriculum, thereby meeting individual needs and motivating the learner to participate fully. In essence it is about enabling education to best fit the learner rather than 'one size education fits all'.

A key element of personalised learning is to ensure that all learners are provided with the support to enable them to achieve, and where necessary with additional lessons and activities to allow the learner to fulfil their potential and thus achieve their goals. As a concept personalised learning is seen as being crucial in helping our young people to progress and achieve while at the same time it is raising standards and aspirations. The underpinning pedagogy is the expectation that all learners will reach or exceed the national expectations for their age and ability levels. As a consequence the most important element within personalised learning is an effective process to monitor the learner and their progress to ensure that their learning is meaningful, challenging and allows them to succeed, together with appropriate target setting for the learner. An effective ILP will allow this to happen.

However, personalised learning is not just linked to the ILP but can also be linked to the learning, teaching and assessment that you use within your programmes, which in turn can be integrated into the ILP. As a diploma teacher, providing an effective personalised learning approach will ensure that you meet the needs of all your learners, either through providing the relevant support or providing the extension needed to further learner thinking and develop higher-level skills.

As a concept it is my belief that the ILP is central to personalised learning and an effective model would be as shown in Figure 5.1.

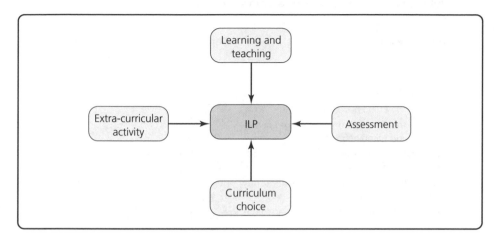

Figure 5.1 Suggested components of an effective ILP

Why not try this?

Consider a recent session that you have delivered to your 14–19 year olds.

Select two of the learners from the class. What learning, teaching and assessment strategies could you integrate into their ILP to ensure that they continue to be motivated, challenged and supported on the route to achieving their individual goal?

Reflecting on practice

Phillip has chosen to study a Level 3 diploma in construction and the built environment. His ultimate goal is to work as a town and country planner within a local authority. His principal learning and generic learning is provided in the table below. He has made an appointment to see you as his tutor regarding his additional or specialist learning and with a view to building his individual learning plan.

Consider the following:

1. Where could you find information regarding additional or specialist learning?

2. What other information services could you signpost him to for further information?

Phillip's principal and generic learning choices

Principal learning	Generic learning	Additional specialist learning
7 mandatory units • Design the Built Environment: design factors • Design the Built Environment: stages in the design and planning process • Design the Built Environment: physical and environmental influences • Create the Built Environment: health, safety and environmental influences • Create the Built Environment: management processes • Value and Use of the Built Environment: adding value in the wider community • Value and Use of the Built Environment: protecting and maintaining	3 × functional skills qualifications at Level 2 (80 guided learning hourist GLH) Level 3 project qualification (60 GLH) 10 days work experience Personal, learning and thinking skills (60 GLH)	

Conclusion

Information, advice and guidance is an essential element of all young people's learning, particularly so in the diplomas as learners will need to be signposted to the most appropriate additional elements that will enhance their programme and provide progression opportunities. As a process IAG should be seen as a collaboration between careers advisers, schools, colleges, employers and other relevant bodies and not just a process that is undertaken by one individual.

Key ideas summary

- Information, advice and guidance is a key responsibility for the 14–19 teacher.

- Where might you find information regarding advice for your learners?

- Who else could you refer your learners to?

- What information should you include in an ILP?

- Who should have ownership of the ILP?

- What are the advantages for you in developing an ILP with your learners?

Going further

CIBT (2009) *A Follow-up Study of New Arrangements for Connexions/ Careers/ IAG Services for Young People in England.*

DCSF (2007) Education and Skills Bill, London: DCSF.

DCSF (2008) *Quality Standards for Young People's Information, Advice and Guidance (IAG)*, London: DCSF.

DfES (2004) *Delivering Skills for Life: The Learning Journey*, London: DfES.

Gilbert, C. (2007) *2020 Vision. Report of the Teaching and Learning in 2020 Review Group*, www.teachernet.gov.uk

Miliband, D. (2004) www.standards.dfes.gov.uk/personalisedlearning

Ofsted (2006) *The Common Inspection Framework for Inspecting post-16 Education and Training*, London: Ofsted.

Ofsted (2009) *Implementation of 14–19 Reforms, Including the Introduction of Diplomas*, London: Ofsted.

www.excellencegateway.org.uk – Excellence Gateway.

Personal learning and thinking skills

What this chapter will explore:

- Background of the personal, learning and thinking skills framework
- Overview of the framework and the learner focus
- Unpacking the skills
- Ideas for integrating PLTS
- Awarding bodies and PLTS assessment
- Assessment and recording principles for PLTS

Personal learning and thinking skills (PLTS) are as indicated above a new set of skills that all diploma learners must achieve within their qualification. They have been designed to help our young people to gain the necessary skills to enter the adult world, whether they begin employment or move on to higher education. This chapter will examine the PLTS and how they can be assessed within the diploma classroom.

'The personal, learning and thinking skills (PLTS) provide a framework for describing the qualities and skills needed for success in learning and life.'

(QCA, 2009)

What are personal learning and thinking skills (PLTS)?

The Qualifications and Curriculum Authority believe that for our learners and young people to be successful in their future they need to develop some skills that are deemed to be essential for learning, life and employment. The PLTS framework has been developed to complement the functional skills discussed in Chapter 4 and to provide a range of skills that equip our young learners for the future. Within the diploma lines the students need to successfully complete the PLTS in order to be awarded the qualification.

The six PLTS are:

1. Independent enquirers.
2. Creative thinkers.
3. Reflective learners.
4. Team workers.
5. Self-managers.
6. Effective participators.

For each group of skills there is a focus statement that identifies the main personal, learning and thinking skills in that group. Each skill group although distinctive can also be interconnected. For example, learners are likely to encounter a range of different skills from different groups in each activity or learning experience. Each skill groups' focus statement is followed by a set of outcome statements that are indicative of behaviours and personal qualities associated with each group. These skills should be embedded into the teaching of the diploma lines and form an integral element of the teaching and learning of the subject.

Overview of the PLTS framework

The PLTS framework is set out by the QCA (2007a) and although designed to be a framework to develop the skills of young learners it could also be argued that as a reference point it is equally important in any area of learning. The framework is reproduced here in full to allow you to consider the overall links between the different skills before we look at each skill in more detail and identify how they can be used in diploma teaching.

Independent enquirers
Focus:
Young people process and evaluate information in their investigations, planning what to do and how to go about it. They take informed and well-reasoned decisions, recognising that others have different beliefs and attitudes.

Young people:
identify questions to answer and problems to resolve, plan and carry out research, appreciating the consequences of decisions explore issues, events or problems from different perspectives analyse and evaluate information, judging its relevance and value
consider the influence of circumstances, beliefs and feelings on decisions and events
support conclusions, using reasoned arguments and evidence

Creative thinkers
Focus:
Young people think creatively by generating and exploring ideas, making original connections. They try different ways to tackle a problem, working with others to find imaginative solutions and outcomes that are of value.

Young people:
generate ideas and explore possibilities
ask questions to extend their thinking
connect their own and others' ideas and experiences in inventive ways
question their own and others' assumptions
try out alternatives or new solutions and follow ideas through
adapt ideas as circumstances change

Reflective learners
Focus:
Young people evaluate their strengths and limitations, setting themselves realistic goals with criteria for success. They monitor their own performance and
progress, inviting feedback from others and making changes to further their learning.

Young people:
assess themselves and others, identifying opportunities and achievements
set goals with success criteria for their development and work
review progress, acting on the outcomes
invite feedback and deal positively with praise, setbacks and criticism
evaluate experiences and learning to inform future progress
communicate their learning in relevant ways for different audiences

Team workers
Focus:
Young people work confidently with others, adapting to different contexts and taking responsibility for their own part. They listen to and take account of different views.
They form collaborative relationships, resolving issues to reach agreed outcomes.

Young people:
collaborate with others to work towards common goals
reach agreements, managing discussions to achieve results
adapt behaviour to suit different roles and situations, including leadership roles
show fairness and consideration to others
take responsibility, showing confidence in themselves and their contribution
provide constructive support and feedback to others

➔

Self-managers
Focus:
Young people organise themselves, showing personal responsibility, initiative, creativity and enterprise with a commitment to learning and self-improvement. They actively embrace change, responding positively to new priorities, coping with challenges and looking for opportunities.

Young people:
seek out challenges or new responsibilities and show flexibility when priorities change
work towards goals, showing initiative, commitment and perseverance
organise time and resources, prioritising actions
anticipate, take and manage risks
deal with competing pressures, including personal and work-related demands
respond positively to change, seeking advice and support when needed
manage their emotions, and build and maintain relationships.

Effective participators
Focus:
Young people actively engage with issues that affect them and those around them. They play a full part in the life of their school, college, workplace or wider
community by taking responsible action to bring improvements for others as well as themselves.

Young people:
discuss issues of concern, seeking resolution where needed to present a persuasive case for action
propose practical ways forward, breaking these down into manageable steps
identify improvements that would benefit others as well as themselves
try to influence others, negotiating and balancing diverse views to reach workable solutions
act as an advocate for views and beliefs that may differ from their own

It should be noted that time for the application of PLTS within each line of learning is written into the respective units (that is, as learning outcomes and associated content) within the guided learning hours (GLH) that have been allocated to the principal learning. These GLH are intended to specifically support the learning and development of PLTS at each level of diploma.

Providers of each diploma line must ensure that the diploma includes the relevant opportunities to develop and apply all six personal, learning and thinking skills within principal learning. Further opportunities may be offered in work experience and the project.

Unpacking the skills

So what is an independent enquirer and how can these skills be embedded and assessed within the diplomas? If we examine the focuses as identified by the QCA, the first skill, the independent enquirer, is about the learner being able to make reasoned decisions regarding the sources of information that he or she utilises to solve a problem or complete an assessment. The question for teachers is how much guidance we can give our learners before the guidance removes the independent decisions that we are encouraging through this skill. Here QCA (2007b) state that each diploma level should support the PLTS as appropriate and that differentiation between diploma levels should be determined by:

- the amount of support a learner is given;
- the degree of sophistication of the skills used;
- the level of demand of the task, problem or context in which these skills are applied.

As teachers we also need to be aware of the number of guided learning hours within our principal lines of learning as these have been allocated to cover specific PLTS, whereas the guided learning hours identified in the generic learning are to support the development of the PLTS and are not necessarily contextualised to the relevant subject area. When considering PLTS teachers also need to be mindful of the Diploma Development Partnerships (DDP) guidelines for each line of learning.

> **Why not try this?**
>
> Contact your local DDP and download any published guidelines for PLTS.
>
> How might this impact upon your teaching?

Ideas for integrating the skills

The guidelines for the delivery of PLTS within the diploma are very clear. They should be integrated into the assessment for the principal learning and not treated as an additional subject to be bolted on to the principal learning.

The following sections provide some ideas for embedding PLTS into the diploma.

Independent enquirers

The essence of an independent enquirer is the ability to take full responsibility for their learning, the way in which they learn and the final outcome of the learning. As a skill it links well with the skills of creative thinking, reflection and self-management and for teachers it provides many opportunities to engage and motivate the learner by allowing them to connect a subject area with their own individual beliefs and experiences. How then do we encourage the learner to become an independent enquirer?

Edward de Bono's Six Thinking Hats is one way in which we can encourage the learner to focus on the enquiry process. The idea enables the learner to consider different approaches to a problem, or to consider the different types of thought processes needed to solve a problem or issue. As a strategy the Six Thinking Hats can be used as a tool within group activities to help learners formulate questions, explore issues, events or problems from different perspectives and analyse and evaluate information, judging its relevance and value. See Figure 6.1.

The White Hat
White Hat thinking focuses on data, facts, information known or needed.

The Black Hat
Black Hat thinking focuses on difficulties, potential problems. Why something may not work.

The Red Hat
Red Hat thinking focuses on feelings, hunches, gut instinct and intuition.

The Green Hat
Green Hat thinking focuses on creativity: possibilities, alternatives, solutions, new ideas.

The Yellow Hat
White Hat thinking focuses on values and benefits. Why something may work.

The Blue Hat
Blue Hat thinking focuses on managing the thinking process, focus, next steps, action plans.

Figure 6.1 de Bono's Six Thinking Hats

Source: www.debonoconsulting.com/six_thinking_hats.asp, reproduced with permission from De Bono Global

Why not try this?

You have asked your learners to plan an event that allows them to collect money for a local charity, while at the same time providing them with the opportunity to work in teams to meet part of the learning outcomes for the applied learning within your diploma line.

How could you best use the Six Thinking Hats to encourage independent enquiry?

Another useful tool for teachers wishing to encourage independent enquiry is the enquiry wheel, which allows the learner to see the generic stages of the process of enquiry, while at the same time providing the information that they may need to think through the process.

As a tool the enquiry wheel has many advantages for both the teacher and the learner. For example, it provides a visual and explicit teaching tool to help the learner understand the process of independent enquiry, while at the same time providing an overview of a learner's development. For the learner it can help provide a stronger focus for the task in question, while also allowing them to identify their own strengths and areas for development.

An example of an enquiry wheel is available from www.teachingexpertise.com/ebulletins/developing_independent_enquirers_how_struture_enquiry_3456.

Creative thinkers

As discussed earlier in this chapter the concept of creative thinkers is that they generate ideas and explore possibilities, ask questions to extend their thinking, connect their own and others' ideas and experiences in inventive ways, question their own and others' assumptions, try out alternatives or new solutions and follow ideas through, and adapt their ideas as circumstances change. So how can this skill be encouraged and developed? Petty (1996) discusses one approach that may be of use within the classroom as being the ICEDIP model. This model outlines six key phases that a learner passes through when developing creativity, although these phases are in no particular order and may be revisited at any stage throughout the process. The six phases are: inspiration, clarification, evaluation, distillation, incubation and perspiration (ICEDIP) as shown in the table below (adapted from Petty, 1996).

ICEDIP phases

Phase	Activity	Characteristics
Inspiration	Generation of a large number of ideas	Sponateous, experimental, intuitive, risk taking
Clarification	Focus on goals	Questioning, clarifying goals
Evaluation	Review of work in progress	SWOT, improvement
Distillation	Evaluation of ideas and decision making	Self-critique, evaluative
Incubation	Leave work alone	Subconscious time
Perspiration	Work on ideas	Determination

Using the ICEDIP model to assess and log creative skills

One of the ways the ICEDIP model can be used effectively in the classroom is to set a challenge for your learners that they must work through to achieve a given outcome. At the end of the process introduce the ICEDIP phases and ask the learners to identify each of the stages that they went through when completing the challenge. What were the strengths? What areas do they need to develop?

Reflective learners

In order to be reflective learners our young people need to understand the process of reflection and its importance in the learning cycle. Several definitions and approaches of reflection exist. Moon (2004, p 82) describes reflection as 'akin to thinking but with more added to it'. She further explains this as a common-sense approach to reflection on what happened, what went well, what went poorly, what others did/said and what you then did after that. To take this approach could be as simple as asking our learners to describe how they approached a particular task, which could be done in writing, verbally, as a video or pod cast or as a blog diary entry. Activities that lend themselves to this reflection include group presentations or the delivery of an event of some description.

Why not try this?

Revisit a recent activity that you asked your learners to complete within the classroom situation.

1. Task 1: Ask the learner to complete an individual SWOT analysis on their performance, concentrating on the following areas:

Strengths	Weaknesses (areas for development)
– What did I do well?	– What did I do badly?
– Which areas am I strongest at? (knowledge/expertise)	– What are my weaknesses? (knowledge/expertise)
Opportunities (for me)	**Threats (to me and the performance)**
– What is my strength?	– What were the problems?
– What else might I have done?	– What could have affected me?

2. Task 2: In small groups (non-threatening) encourage the learners to complete a SWOT for each other.

3. Task 3: Allow learners to compare and contrast the results from the individual and peer SWOT.

4. Task 4: Ask the learner to formally record the two SWOTS in whatever format they prefer.

Schon (1983) takes a different approach to reflection and discusses reflection-in-action and reflection-on-action. The former refers to changes being made as things happen, the latter being the reflection after a change has been made. It could be suggested that reflection-in-action is a higher-order skill as it relies on a learner being able to identify when things are going wrong and 'thinking on their feet' to make changes. Regardless of the approach to reflection that you take with learners the use of reflective practice can be a very effective tool to help learners self-improve, as it allows them to consider their performance on a variety of levels, from an academic viewpoint to a social viewpoint when working with others. It can, if embedded effectively, produce autonomy amongst our learners while improving and strengthening their knowledge of the subject matter. Roffey-Barentsen and Malthouse (2009) highlight the following as being characteristics of a reflective practice approach:

● makes use of a reflective practice cycle (Kolb,1984; Gibbs, 1988);

● makes use of analysis in its recording;

● links to previous works;

● can be recorded as a formal document;

● can be individual but can also make use of input from others;

● is developmental;

● can be aspirational for the learner.

Team workers

Team working as a skill relies on members of a learning group to cooperate and work together effectively for a common purpose. The ethos of team working is that all team members are interdependent upon each other while at the same time having individual accountability and equal participation. Various barriers exist to effective team working, for example dominant students, shy students and personality clashes within the group. Therefore to encourage effective teamwork the teacher needs to ensure a degree of collaboration and cooperation between group members. One strategy for encouraging this is to identify group roles and strengths at an early stage. One way of doing this is to make use of the Belbin team role constructs that enable a learner to identify their role type and tasks which they are best suited to within the team. (See www.belbin.com for the Belbin questionnaire.) An alternative personality profile that learners can access is the 'big five' factors personality model, which describes the five fundamental factors of an individual's personality, together with an analysis of their typical behaviours.

Self-managers and effective participators

As can be seen in the QCA framework at the beginning, self-management skills involve learners seeking out challenges or new responsibilities; being flexible; showing initiative, commitment and perseverance; prioritising actions; anticipating, taking and managing risks; seeking advice and support when needed; managing their emotions; and building and maintaining relationships, while effective participators discuss issues of concern, seeking resolution where needed; present a persuasive case for action; propose practical ways forward, breaking these down into manageable steps; identify improvements that would benefit others as well as themselves; and try to influence others, negotiating and balancing diverse views to reach workable solutions.

All of these skills can also be embedded into teamwork and independent enquiry and as such should be included within the same strategies that are being used to address these skills.

Why not try this?

Taking either de Bono's Six Thinking Hats, ICEDIP or the wheel of enquiry as a basis, map the focus statements of self-managers and effective participators on to the model.

How could you use this new extended model within your classroom?

Assessing and recording PLTS

Awarding bodies involved with the diploma have generally integrated the PLTS within the assessment criteria of each unit within the principal learning, and therefore any assessment is automatically embedded within the programme itself.

Why not try this?

Download the specification for your particular line of learning.

Create a table to highlight where each of the PLTS and their associated focuses are assessed within the principal learning.

Design a tracking sheet to track achievement of the PLTS for your learners

In recording PLTS the QCA, together with diploma developers and stakeholders, have identified a range of general principles for recording the achievement of PLTS. The main aim of providing general principles is to ensure that there is a consistent approach across both lines of learning and the various consortia delivering the diplomas. These principles are reproduced here in full, and are available at www.qca.org.uk.

TOP TIP!

All diploma learners, at all levels, should be encouraged to develop and should be provided with support in recording PLTS.

The primary purpose of recording PLTS should be to inform and support skill recognition and development.

The recording process should be relevant and meaningful to the learner, and owned by the learner.

Recording should be part of the diploma planning and review process, to aid reflection on PLTS, recognise progress and achievements, and to inform discussions on ways to further develop these skills.

The form and frequency of PLTS recording should be manageable for learners and teachers, and take account of other systems in place within the centre/consortium.

Access to and use of a PLTS record should be determined by the learner.

The PLTS recording process and output of the recording should be subject to monitoring and evaluation to ensure quality of provision and equality of access.

However, despite the publication of the general principles, autonomy still exists within each consortia to develop a system that is the most appropriate for their learners, delivery methods and consortia stakeholders. Different learners and different qualification levels will need different levels of support, depending upon previous experience and skills. One way of recording and identifying learner needs could be within the individual learning plans and initial advice and guidance sessions. It is at this point that one of the key questions about recording is raised, that is, who within the consortia will be responsible for the recording of PLTS and how will the consortia ensure that all of the PLTS are covered without unnecessary duplication. This becomes even more problematic when we consider the general principle that the access to and use of a record should be determined by the learner. Several methods of recording have been adapted throughout the piloting process of PLTS and two case studies are available at www.qca.org.uk/14-19/11-16schools.

Conclusion

The six personal, learning and thinking skills are central to the diploma qualification and they need to be achieved for the learner to get the qualification, at whatever level. The differentiation between diploma levels should be determined by:

- the amount of support a learner is given;
- the degree of sophistication of the skills used;
- the level of demand of the task, problem or context in which these skills are applied.

Most awarding bodies have embedded the assessment of the skills into the principal learning of the qualification but it is the diploma consortia that have the task of recording their achievement through the development of a recording process in line with the general principles as developed by the QCA.

Key ideas summary

- How can I best introduce PLTS?
- How can I encourage my learners to take ownership of PLTS?
- What are the best models for assessing skills within the classroom for my learners?
- What are the most effective recording processes and tools for my learners?

- How can I ensure that the recording tools used enable the learners to develop?

- How will the recording of PLTS be disseminated across the partnership?

Going further

de Bono, E. (1985) *Six Thinking Hats*, London: Penguin.

Gibbs, G. (1988) *Learning by Doing*, London: Further Education Unit.

Kolb, J.A. (1984) *Experiential Learning: Experience as the Source of Learning and Development,* Houston, TX: Gulf Publishing.

Moon, J. (2004) *A Handbook of Reflective and Experiential Learning Theory and Practice*, London: Routledge.

Petty, G. (1996) *How to be Better at Creativity*, London: Kogan Page.

Petty, G. (2006) *Evidence Based Teaching: A Practical Approach*, Cheltenham: Nelson Thornes.

QCA (2007a) www.curriculum.qcda.org.uk

QCA (2007b) www.qcda.gov.uk

QCA (2009) http://curriculum.qcda.gov.uk/key_stages_3_and_4/skills/plts

Roffey-Barentsen, J. and Malthouse, R. (2009) *Reflective Practice in the Lifelong Learning Sector*, Exeter: Learning Matters.

Schon, D.A. (1983) *The Reflective Practitioner*, New York: Basic Books.

www.belbin.com – Belbin questionnaire.

www.businessballs.com/personalitystylesmodels.htm

www.enquiringminds.org.uk

www.futurelab.org.uk/resources/documents/project_reports/Developing_and _ accrediting_ personal_skills) and_competencies.pdf

www.qca.org.uk

www.qca.org.uk/14-19/11-16schools – PLTS recording case studies.

www.teachingexpertise.com/ebulletins/developing_independent_ enquirers/_how_structure_enquiry_3456 – example of an enquiry wheel.

Reflective practice

What this chapter will explore:

- What is reflective practice?
- Why is reflective practice important for the diploma teacher and student?
- The reflective practice process
- Models of reflective practice
- Recording reflection
- Linking reflective practice and the personal learning and thinking skills

This chapter will discuss the concept of reflective practice and how it can be used with the 14–19 learner. Various reflective practice models will be discussed and examples of reflection in action provided.

'A reflection in a mirror is an exact replica of what is in front of it. Reflection in practice, however, gives back not what it is, but what it might be, an improvement on the original.'

(Biggs,1999, p 6)

What is reflective practice?

Moon defines reflective practice as 'a set of abilities and skills, to indicate the taking of a critical stance, an orientation to problem solving or state of mind' (1999, p 63). The Higher Education Academy defines it as 'an approach that promotes autonomous learning that aims to develop students' understanding and critical thinking skills' (www.ukle.ac.uk, accessed 20 July 2009). As discussed in Chapter 6 we have already seen that reflective practice can take several different approaches, the first being reflection on a particular situation in terms of what happened, who did what, and how you felt about it (common-sense reflecting). The second approach is taking common-sense reflection one step further, through learning from the reflection to improve and develop (reflective thinking), and the third being reflection in action and reflection on action (reflective practice). Reflection in action being the reflection that takes place during a particular activity and reflection on action being the reflection completed at the end of a particular activity (Schon, 1983).

Why not try this?

Consider the last group activity you took part in, either within the work situation or in a social situation.

Taking the three types of reflection described above jot down a few notes under each heading.

Which did you find the easiest to do?

Which parts did you find difficult?

Within the teaching profession reflective practice as a process is a professional requirement and all teachers, at some stage in their development, will have to provide evidence that they are reflective practitioners, usually in the form of a reflective journal or reflective log. Most introductory teacher training programmes, whether for secondary or lifelong learning, include reflection as an integral part of the teachers' development. In addition, many of the professional bodies related to teaching require their members to reflect upon their practice for continuous improvement.

The Institute for Learning, the professional body responsible for teachers in the life-long learning sector, have as part of their commitment to reflection introduced an online tool for their members to enable them to record and critically reflect upon professional development activities, share good practice and assess the impact that any professional development has on practice.

Why not try this?

Consider the professional organisations that you belong to.

How do they encourage reflection?

You may wish to consider some or all of the following: Higher Education Academy (HEA), General Teaching Council (GTC), Institute for Learning (IFL), Chartered Institute of Educational Assessors (CIEA), and any subject professional organisation that you may belong to.

Why reflect?

As a teacher there are several reasons for reflection, the most obvious being because we have to! However, it would be foolish to think that this is the most important reason, as reflective practice can be very beneficial to the individual.

Roffey-Barentsen and Malthouse (2009) identify ten benefits of reflective practice for the teacher:

1. Improvement of teaching.
2. Learning from reflection.
3. Enhancing problem-solving skills.
4. Enabling critical thinking.
5. Enabling decision making.
6. Improving organisational skills.
7. Managing personal change.
8. Acknowledging personal values.
9. Listening and taking self-advice.
10. Recognising emancipatory benefits.

Let's have a look at each of these in turn and identify how they may benefit our diploma learner.

Improvement of teaching: obviously reflective practice is not going to improve our diploma learners' teaching! However, if we consider the underlying concept of this benefit what we are actually doing by encouraging our learners to reflect is enabling them to improve their individual practice. This practice may be their learning, the completion of a particular task or activity, or the way they work in group situations. Regardless of what they are trying to improve reflective practice is a powerful tool that you can use in the classroom and can be one of the most effective teaching and learning methods available to you.

The second benefit identified above is that of *learning from reflection*. Moon (2004) considers the link between learning and reflection and refers to a continuum of learning, with a surface approach to learning on one end and a deep approach on the other. Learners taking a deep approach to learning are analysing and making links between knowledge to evaluate and transfer knowledge gained to other situations. In other words they are using a higher degree of reflection to enable them to learn. Figure 7.1 demonstrates how increased reflection encourages increased learning.

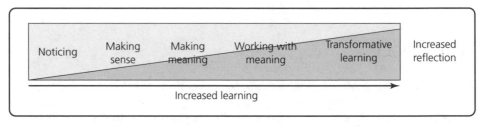

Figure 7.1 Type of learning related to the amount of reflection undertaken

Source: Adapted from Moon (2004), p 85. Reprinted with permission

Reflecting on practice

Consider the Diploma in Construction and the Built Environment, Level 2, Unit 1, Design the Built Environment: The design process. In this unit a learner needs to demonstrate that they can compare and contrast the way in which different service utilities are used within design.

They are required to identify a range of primary service utilities (gas, electricity, water, etc.), describe how they are installed and how decisions are made about installation locations, and consider any impact on the environment.

Taking the five elements that Moon features in Figure 7.1 explain the process a learner would go through when working towards this learning outcome.

Enhancing problem solving skills: most diploma lines will involve some element of problem solving, even if in its simplest form the problem to be solved is, 'How do

I complete this assessment?' Reflection will enable the learner to consider the most appropriate way in which to approach a task or activity. Many learners will go through the problem-solving process without realising that they have done so, although some learners may need prompting.

> **TOP TIP!**
>
> *When you next give your group an activity or tasks to complete give them a prompt sheet to work through before they actually start the task. The prompt sheet should allow them to consider four questions:*
>
> *What is the task? (clarification)*
>
> *What are the possible issues/problems? (analysis)*
>
> *What could I do? (deliberation)*
>
> *What shall I do? (selection)*
>
> *Following the completion of the task the learner should then be encouraged to consider the final question:*
>
> *Did it work? (evaluation).*

For the learner the benefits of *critical thinking* and *decision making* appear to be synonymous with problem solving, in that decision making is part of the problem-solving process. Our learners will have to make a decision as to which of the possible options available to them should be used. The critical-thinking element comes in when the learners are able to make informed judgements, based on all of the available information, rejecting information that is incomplete, incorrect or not appropriate. Not all of our learners will be adept at critical thinking. However, reflection can help improve this skill by allowing the learner the time to consider, analyse and then make decisions.

Organisational skills tend to be skills that many young people have difficulty with, as prioritising their personal lives above that of school or college is often more tempting. However, the diploma qualifications require the learner to have some degree of organisational and self-management skills to complete the extended project elements. It is here in particular that the ability to self-manage becomes important as learners are required to plan their project in advance. If we look at the guidelines for the Level 2 project the assessment comprises of a project proposal form, a production log, a written report detailing the sources of information and research (links to problem solving and decision making), evidence of project completion and a presentation. Without the ability to manage their own time effectively a learner will not be able to complete this. As the teacher you can help with encouraging time management and self-reflection through the ILP and action planning processes discussed in Chapter 5.

Managing personal change, acknowledging personal values and listening and taking self-advice are the skills that a learner may find most difficult to reconcile as managing personal change relies on a learner being able to look inward and analyse their own thoughts and feelings while being aware of others around them. This form of reflection can sometimes lead to negativity, with the learner becoming convinced that they are inadequate and incapable of completing the tasks set. Other learners may react differently and, rather than believing themselves inadequate, blame the teacher for their not being able to complete the task. They haven't been taught, the teacher was rubbish, it's a waste of time, are things that you may hear in your classroom. The art of self-reflection encourages the learner to change their perceptions and in so doing change their attitudes towards the tasks in hand, taking advice from both their inner self and from others, while acknowledging that everyone has a right to their opinions. Harris and Harris (1986) sum up this acknowledgement in the following table.

I'm OK	I'm OK
You're OK	You're not OK
I'm not OK	I'm not OK
You're OK	You're not OK

The quadrant to strive for is I'm OK, You're OK, as here the learner accepts both his or her own values and those of others equally. I'm OK, You're not OK indicates that the learner thinks that they are right and everyone else is wrong. I'm not OK, You're OK indicates that the learner is insecure and looks to others for support and guidance regardless of their own feelings, and the final box, I'm not OK, You're not OK indicates a situation where a learner sees both themselves and others as worthless.

Finally, *recognising emancipatory benefits*, allows our learners to take control of their own learning, while recognising the limitations of themselves as individuals.

So in conclusion why should we encourage our diploma learners to use reflective practice? As a tool, reflective practice allows us to understand our needs and abilities and if encouraged can enable learners to improve their own learning, develop self-awareness and can help with the PLTS skill of self-management.

The reflective practice process

Models of reflective practice

Most models of the reflective practice process are presented as cyclical, and this section will explore some of these models and how they can be used to encourage reflection in the classroom. This list is not intended to be exhaustive and information on further reading is supplied at the end of the chapter.

The simplest model is that of Greenaway (2002), which is based on a three-stage model of *plan*, *do*, *review*, based on the quality improvement cycle found in business. If we use this model in the classroom we are effectively using common-sense reflection as described by Moon (1999). What it fails to include is the learning element from the review; however, as a starting point it is a useful model to encourage the learner to use as a basis to build upon. It can be used with a series of 'what' questions based around the description of what happened, without the learner making any judgements or evaluation. For example, What did you do? What happened? What went wrong?

Why not try this?

Consider a recent activity that your learners have completed as a class exercise.

Devise a set of common-sense reflection questions that they can complete to reflect upon the exercise.

The second model that you can use is the four-stage model that takes the Greenaway model one step further and includes the element of drawing conclusions. The most well-known model here is that of Kolb, which is described in more detail in Chapter 2. Essentially this model of reflection is based on experiential learning and relies on the learner planning, doing, reviewing and drawing conclusions before repeating the cycle. This model not only questions the 'what' within an event but expands this by asking 'why' to evaluate and analyse the event. See Figure 7.2.

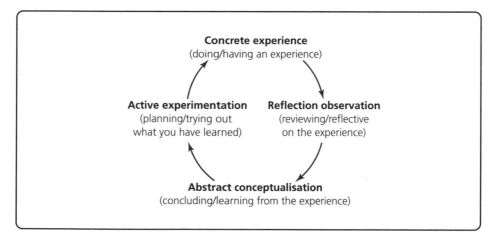

Figure 7.2 Basic reflective cycle

Source: Copyright 2007 David A. Kolb, Experience Based Learning Systems, Inc. Reprinted with permission from the Hay Group, Inc. (www.haygroup.com)

> ## Why not try this?
>
> Consider a recent example from your own teaching within the diploma. Using the four-stage model identified by Kolb consider the session and how you would develop it based on your reflection.
>
> How could you use this model in the classroom?

The final model of reflection that will be explored here is the six-stage model of reflection provided by Gibbs (1988) and based upon the model of learning by doing. This model is shown in Figure 7.3.

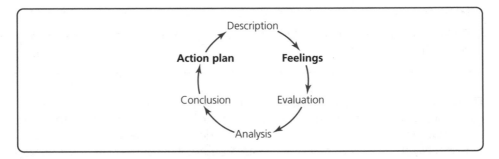

Figure 7.3 Kolb reflective cycle

Source: Adapted from Gibbs (1988). Reprinted with permission

This model makes the process of reflective practice more complete through the explicit need for the reflective process to include action plans that will inform future learning. In unpacking this process Gibbs provides a series of questions that can be used with the learner (see Figure 7.4).

Other writers discuss the elements of this process further. Roffey-Barentsen and Malthouse (2009) describe the SHARK mnemonic guide to help the learner focus on the elements of the cycle:

S Saw

H Heard

A Action

R Result

K Knowledge

Try this with your learners. Does it help them focus more effectively in the experience or activity?

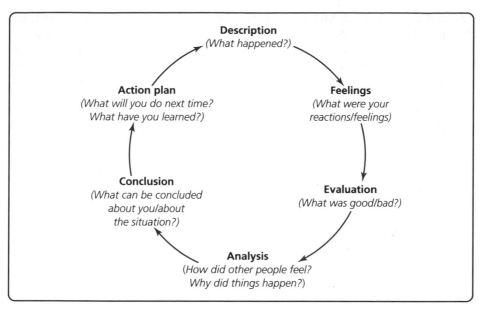

Figure 7.4 Gibbs reflective cycle

Source: Adapted from Gibbs (1988). Reprinted with permission

Recording reflection

The process of reflection can help our learners to develop from being inexperienced and lacking in confidence to becoming experienced and confident learners. Many of the skills that the learner gains along his or her path will become second nature. Consider the unaccredited model shown below (Figure 7.5), sometimes referred to as Hertzberg steps, which suggests that we move through a series of stages aided by the process of reflection.

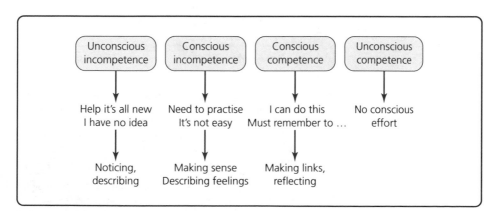

Figure 7.5 'Hertzberg steps'

When discussing this model the most common analogy used to explain the levels is that of learning to drive. A completely new learner will have no concept of the requirements of driving, yet move through to it becoming second nature, where they do not have to consciously think about what they are doing – it is automatic. If we relate this to our learners in short what we are aiming for is that the learner will eventually have:

> 'The wealth of knowledge and routines that they employ, in fact, so automatic that they often do not realise why they preferred a certain plan of action over another. However, when questioned, they are able to reconstruct the reasons for their decisions and behaviour.'

(Rollett, 2001, p 27)

So how should we encourage our learners to record their reflection and reflective practice? If we insist on our learners recording absolutely everything we may run the risk of creating a negative attitude towards reflection. We need to find a balance that allows the learner to take ownership of reflection while at the same time attributing value to the process.

Here are a few ideas, together with possible advantages and disadvantages, that you may wish to consider within your own practice.

Tool	Advantages	Disadvantages
Reflective diary	Can be in many different formats, e.g. written, pictorial, online. Learner has ownership	Ensuring they are completed effectively could remove own ership
Blog	Personalised, individual	Ownership issues
Reflective writing submitted with each task	Can be assessed easily	Could become a chore
ILP	A learner can see their progress easily. Is personal to the learner, the learner has ownership	Reality of ownership (see Chapter 5)
Scrapbook and Post-its	Allows learner to reflect immediately	Post-its being mislaid
Video/audio recording	Personal, but can also work well with group reflection	Time consuming. Reluctance of students to participate
Observation and questioning following an activity	Can direct the learner to reflect more effectively.	Teacher led
Group discussion	Encourages an element of peer reflection into the process	Less confident students may not feel able to participate

Reflection and the personal learning and thinking skills

Regardless of how we choose to encourage reflection amongst our learners we need to ensure that the process enables them to achieve the PLTS of reflective learner in which they are required to evaluate their strengths and limitations, set themselves realistic goals with criteria for success and monitor their own performance and progress, inviting feedback from others and making changes to further their learning. The following case study demonstrates how a learner can achieve these PLTS through following an effective process of reflection throughout their learning.

Reflecting on practice

Helen's Journal – Case study scenario

In class today we have been discussing customer service and how we should present ourselves to our customers and colleagues, ready for our assignment on how to carry out customer service effectively.

The first thing that took me by surprise was the range of situations I might find myself in when I start my career in the hospitality industry; I just thought it was cooking! I never realised that there was such a variety of jobs and organisations within the industry. I decided that I would make myself a checklist of the different types of jobs and the possible customer face-to-face situations that there might be.

I found this quite easy but the teacher said that I hadn't thought about different types of customers and their needs. I knew that I would need some extra help with this part so I arranged to speak to a receptionist at a local hotel. She was really helpful and talked to me about people with disabilities, overseas visitors, families, couples, and lots of other types of visitors that I hadn't even thought of! For example, I never knew that hotels could provide special bread for people with gluten intolerance. I didn't even know what gluten intolerance was!

After my meeting with the hotel receptionist I went back to my checklist and added more information on different customer types. I feel quite pleased with my list and feel that it will make me more confident when I have to deal with a real customer in my work experience.

Consider the following:

1. Analyse Helen's approach to reflection. What models did she use?
2. How could she have reflected differently to better incorporate the PLTS?
3. Produce a set of guidelines for your learners who choose to use written reflection as a means of reflecting.

Conclusion

Reflective practice as a process can help our learners put their learning into context by encouraging them to make links between the classroom and the real-life situation. It can be used as a method of self-improvement, enabling learners to consider their performances both from an academic perspective and also a personal perspective. There is no right or wrong way to reflect and it should be each individual's personal choice on how to record their reflections, after all it is their own development and achievements that allow them to move from inexperienced to experienced and confident learners.

Key ideas summary

- How can I encourage effective reflection in my classroom?
- What models of reflection will help my learners to focus on their self-development?
- What methods of recording reflection are most appropriate for my learners?
- How can I link their reflection to the PLTS?

Going further

Banks, F. and Shelton Mayes, A. (eds) *Early Professional Development for Teachers*, London: David Fulton.

Biggs, J. and Collins, K. (1982) *Evaluating the Quality of Learning: The SOLO Taxonomy,* New York: Academic Press.

Biggs, J. (1999) *Teaching for Quality Learning at University*, Buckingham: Open University.

Bolton, G. (2005) *Reflective Practice: Writing and Professional Development,* London: Sage.

Gibbs, G. (1988) *Learning by Doing*, London: Further Education Unit.

Greenaway, R. (2002) 'Experiential learning cycles and critiques personal development', Theory and practice in managment training, www.reviewing.co.uk

Harris, T.A. and Harris, A.B. (1986) *Staying OK*, London: Pan.

Kolb, D.A. (1976) *The Learning Style Inventory*, Boston, MA: McBer.

Kolb, D.A. (1984) *Experiential Learning: Experience as the Source of Learning and Development*, Englewood Cliffs, NJ: Prentice Hall, Inc.

Moon, J. (1999) *Reflection in Learning and Personal Development*, London: Kogan Page.

Moon, J. (2004) *A Handbook of Reflective and Experiential Learning Theory and Practice*, London: Routledge.

Roffey-Barentsen, J. and Malthouse, R. (2009) *Reflective Practice in the Lifelong Learning Sector*, Exeter: Learning Matters.

Rollett, B.A. (2001) *How Do Expert Teachers View Themselves?*, in Banks F. and Shelton Mayes, A. (eds) *Early Professional Development for Teachers*, London: David Fulton.

Schon, D.A. (1983) *The Reflective Practitioner*, New York: Basic Books.

www.ukle.ac.uk

Effective mentoring

What this chapter will explore:

- The differences between tutors, mentors, coaches and counsellors
- Definitions of mentoring
- Three dimensions of mentoring
- Mentoring models
- Mentoring skills
- How to be a good mentor for your learners – mentoring relationships
- Peer mentoring
- Mentoring v. coaching
- Benefits of mentoring
- Ethical considerations and mentoring

This chapter will define and discuss the role of tutoring, mentoring, coaching and counselling within a classroom context through the comparison of the roles, the key qualities of each role and their application within the workplace.

'[Mentoring is a] mutually agreeable relationship that is sustained over time and intended to further the professional development of the protégé.'

(www.mentors.net)

What is mentoring?

As a tutor you should be familiar with some of the tasks and responsibilities that form part of the job role. For example, a tutor will work with their learners to set targets, ensuring that those targets stretch the learner in his/her aspirations. They will monitor a learner's progress, overseeing their performance in all aspects of a course, a module or a subject. In this way a tutor is able to identify if a learner is at risk, and provide support to the learner. However, a tutor must be aware of their own competence when providing support and when necessary signpost the learner to other agencies for specialist advice and support. This may be appropriate within initial advice and guidance or when helping a learner make the correct choices for their career aspirations. Green (2001, p 1) defined the tutor as 'central to successful learning'.

If a tutor has these responsibilities what then is the role of the mentor and mentoring within a teaching environment?

As can be seen from the introductory definition to this chapter, mentoring is a process that creates relationships between experienced and less experienced people with a view to helping less experienced person to develop. Other published definitions follow similar themes to this, with Pollard defining mentoring as:

'The provision of support for the learning of one person through the guidance of another person, who is more skilled, knowledgeable and experienced in relation to the context of the learning taking place.'

(Pollard, 1997, p 19)

To put it in its simplest form, a mentor is someone available to learn from.

As teachers most of us will have experienced the benefits of mentoring, or even been a mentor ourselves to trainees or NQTs. As a process it is something that has only recently become formalised within education circles although the concept has been in existence for many years. If we look back at our development as teachers many of us will be able identify someone who was always there to guide us and advise on problems and issues, or to make us feel better when things were not going our way. If we were to look back at the origins of the word mentor, we would see that it first appears in Homer's *Odyssey*, where Mentor, a trusted friend of Odysseus, agrees to look after Odysseus's son while he is away fighting in the Trojan Wars. The word has become an analogy for friend, guardian and adviser.

Why not try this?

What other famous relationships can you think of where one of the people could be identified as being a mentor to the other?

So if a mentor is someone who provides advice and guidance what does this mean for you in the diploma classroom?

Three dimensions of mentoring

Pollard (1997) breaks the actual mentoring role down into three specific areas or dimensions. The first of these dimensions is the structural dimension. This relates to the area in which you are working. Is there anything specific that you need help with regarding the organisation in which you are working, for example rules, regulations, placements, inductions, negotiators? It is likely that you will need to talk to the work placement providers for your students, so what skills will you need there?

The second dimension is that of support, working with the student as a friend or counsellor. This may be to counsel them as to the best way to approach a particular project or problem, or could be as a critical friend helping them with their decision-making process. Look back at Chapter 4, on functional skills. How could you encourage creative thinkers through a mentoring process? The third dimension is that of a professional, training, educating and assessing. In short, what we do on a daily basis to encourage and support our learners to succeed.

Why not try this?

Make a list of the ways in which you will be mentoring your learners throughout their diploma qualification.

You may have come up with some of the following:

- critical friend;
- guiding, advising and supporting;
- providing opportunities;
- practical application;
- listening.

So how can you actually do this in practice? An effective mentor will possess a set of attributes and skills that help them to provide this support to their learners. Let's take a look at some of the skills that you will need.

Mentoring skills

Mentoring skills include the following:

- planning;
- liaising;
- demonstrating;
- facilitating;
- observing;
- assessing;
- guiding;
- questioning;
- listening;
- reflecting.

So what do these mean in practice? Clutterbuck (1985) identified a four-dimensional grid, or positioning map, of ways in which a mentor could support someone. This grid is reproduced as Figure 8.1. You can see from the map that a mentor can position themselves in one of four quadrants between directive and non-directive and challenging and supporting. Dependent upon which quadrant they fall into, they take on a different role. This role is likely to be different with different students, depending upon their needs and level of motivation and commitment. We will come back to this later in this chapter.

Klasen and Clutterbuck (2002) extended this basic grid further and identified what each quadrant means in terms of actual skills. This can be seen in Figure 8.2.

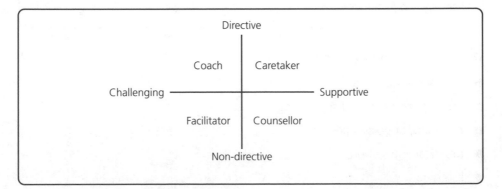

Figure 8.1 Basic mentor support methods

Source: Adapted from Clutterbuck (1985). Reprinted with permission

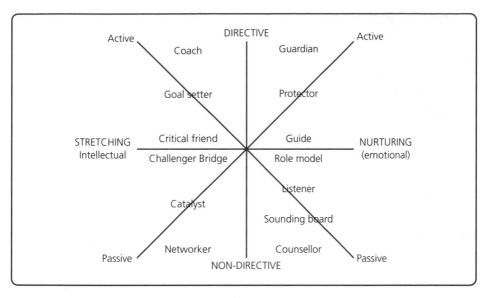

Figure 8.2 Further supportive techniques and skills

Source: Adapted from Klasen and Clutterbuck (2002). Reprinted with permission

Why not try this?

Looking at the list of skills and attributes provided above, plus any others that you have identified, rank in order of importance which skills you would need in Figure 8.2.

Reflect upon these skills and attributes. How do they compare to your own skills and attributes?

What are your own professional development needs in order to be an effective mentor?

Mentoring relationships

The most successful mentoring relationships are relationships that are two-way, both mentor and mentee preparing for and committing to the process.

In addition the mentor and mentee need to be appropriately matched, without any interpersonal issues. This may be a challenge with some of your learners who find it difficult relating to an adult mentor. You may wish to consider peer mentoring (as discussed later in this chapter) as an alternative or supplementary method of supporting these learners.

Top tips for the mentor

No matter which of the skills and quadrants you find yourself working in with a learner it is important to remember the following:

- *For the person being mentored* The quickest way to succeed is to learn from, and to model, people who have made a success of their lives. This could be you, or a famous chef, television presenter, pop star or many others, depending upon the subject area that the learner is studying.

- *For the mentor* The opportunity for self-reflection about their own career path together with an increased understanding of their discipline and its development is a major benefit for a teacher.

Characteristics of a mentor

An effective mentor will help their mentee recognise their own abilities and limitations, while at the same time challenging and encouraging them in their studies. Research published in 2004 by Darwin identified several different characteristics of a mentor. These characteristics, ascribed by their mentees, are divided into eight mentoring dimensions and are reproduced here together with a description of what it means in practice for you as the mentor and for the person you are mentoring. Mentors exhibit behaviours (task and relationship) from all of the eight mentoring dimensions, some more than others.

Defining characteristic	
Authentic	Genuine, fair, honest, supportive, understanding, loyal, helpful, principled, thoughtful, respectful and empowering of others.
Nurturing	Kind, sensitive, compassionate, easy going, spiritual, patient, generous and empathetic to others.
Approachable	Humorous, friendly, encouraging, communicative, positive, open, caring, cooperative and considerate of others.
Competent	Knowledgeable, bright, interested, intelligent, enthusiastic, professional, confident, experienced, insightful and informative to others.
Conscientious	Efficient, organised, disciplined, consistent, strict and available to others.
Hard-working	Dedicated, motivated, committed, ambitious, energetic, driven and workaholics who tend to be demanding of self and others.
Inspirational	Risk-taking, visioning, inspiring, creative, curious, dynamic, strong, passionate, direct, brilliant, challenging and assertive.
Volatile	Neurotic, overbearing, egocentric, outrageous, vindictive, contradictory, self-centred, wild, eccentric, opinionated, stressed, cunning, hard and picky.

Other characteristics include the ability to give feedback to the learner, motivate the learner and to be non-judgemental in the overall approach.

Why not try this?

Revisit your initial reflection of your personal skills and attributes.

What characteristics do you believe you possess based on the above table?

Peer mentoring

Peer mentoring is another form of mentoring that you could make use of within your classroom. As a process peer mentoring is a scheme that allows learners to help each other with their problems, either work related or within the school or college itself. Schools and colleges that have peer mentoring schemes in place use them as a means of improving behaviour, increasing the confidence and self-esteem of the learners and improving relationships amongst students and teachers.

Peer mentors and peer mentoring schemes seem to appear mainly in secondary schools where students moving up from junior/primary schools may need assistance in settling in to the whole new schedule and lifestyle of secondary school. As part of their role a peer mentor can help their mentees with school work and study skills, but have also been used for wider issues, such as attendance, bullying and behavioural issues and/or family problems that a learner may be experiencing.

Although peer mentoring as a term usually applies to learners mentoring learners there is also the opportunity for you to make use of cross-age peer mentoring. This is defined as:

'An interpersonal relationship between different ages that reflects a greater degree of hierarchical power imbalance than is typical of a friendship and in which the goal is for the older to promote one or more aspects of the younger youth's development. It refers to a sustained (long-term), usually formalized (i.e. program-based), developmental relationship. The relationship is 'developmental' in that the older peer's goal is to help guide the younger mentee's development in domains such as interpersonal skills, self-esteem and conventional connectedness and attitudes.'

(DuBois and Karcher, 2005, p 267)

Reflecting on practice

Joel was a boy at the beginning of Year 10. He was considered by all staff to be underachieving within his study, although he showed an aptitude for practical activities. His attendance was poor and the school expected that he would drop out before the end of Key Stage 4. Mentoring was seen as a way of trying to encourage him to work and to motivate him to continue his education.

He was paired with a Year 12 student who had recently undertaken some units on the Level 2 diploma in engineering. The pair worked together on planning his coursework, and the advances that were made, for example a good piece of coursework, helped to improve his self-esteem in areas where he felt less confident.

Consider the following:

1. As the tutor what could you have done to assist this process?

2. What are the benefits for Joel of having a mentor who is only a few years older than him?

3. What would have been the advantages/disadvantages of you as tutor taking on the mentoring role?

Mentoring or coaching?

As a process mentoring is quite often confused with coaching and the words used interchangeably. However, coaching tends to be more of a short-term, task- or project-focused role. It can help individual learners to improve their performance or their personal skills, which in the long term can improve their motivation and confidence within a particular subject. A coach is someone for the performer to work with rather than learn from, as with a mentor. Maclennan (1995, p 4) defines coaching as:

> *'The process whereby one individual helps another; to unlock their natural ability; to perform, to learn, and achieve; to increase awareness of the factors that determine performance; to increase their sense of self-responsibility and ownership of their performance; to self-coach to identify and remove barriers to achievement.'*

As a teacher you will automatically take on the role of coach as you guide your learners to achieve. The ways in which you do this will vary, for example you may just provide a simple checklist for a learner to use as a guide. However, there are several coaching techniques available to you as a teacher.

In this section I would like to explore the concept of coaching and how it could be applied to the classroom in an everyday situation. In every classroom you will have a mix of learners ranging from low ability to high ability, all with varying degrees of commitment to their study and programme.

Why not try this?

Think about your classroom – how many different levels of ability and motivation can you identify, where might they fit within Figure 8.3 below?

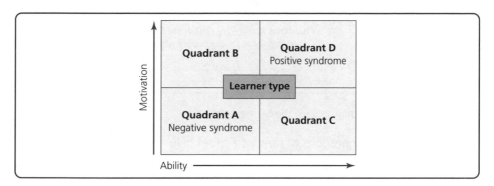

Figure 8.3 Learner types and syndromes

Each quadrant will have learners with different characteristics and therefore the behaviour they may exhibit within your classroom will vary.

● *Quadrant A.* These learners could be described as being in a 'negative syndrome' (Hohman, 2008). They lack ability, whether that be skills or general techniques that they need to succeed, either in the task or the qualification. Furthermore they are not highly motivated to learn, possibly as a result of prior learning experiences, prior failure, or just simply lack of effort.

● *Quadrant B* still has learners with low ability levels, but these learners are more motivated to succeed and try within the classroom. These types of learners will benefit from support as they could very easily fall into quadrant A if their confidence levels fall.

● *Quadrant C* sees the learners being relatively able but not very motivated to succeed. This could be as a result of self doubt in their ability, limited concentration spans, or again, as a result of prior experiences in education.

● *Quadrant D* has the learner who is classed as being in a 'positive syndrome' (Hohman, 2008). The highly motivated, very able student, who is eager to succeed, and confident in their own ability.

All of these quadrants bring their own challenges to you as a teacher and it is important to note that learners may not remain in one particular quadrant, but instead could move from one quadrant to another. Your aim is to have your learners in quadrant D and for them to remain in quadrant D!

As the coach to this diverse and complex range of learners who may change their style and characteristics, you have several different approaches available to you to support their learning.

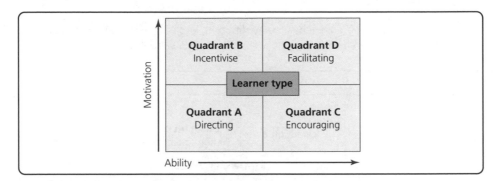

Figure 8.4 Support mechanisms for the learner type

Figure 8.4 provides suggestions of how you could help these learners.

- *Directing*. Here the focus is on supervision and instruction whereby the teacher advises and oversees the learner as they lack the skills and motivation to work unsupervised.

- *Incentivise*. A two-way communication whereby the teacher advises and oversees the learner as they lack the skills and motivation to work unsupervised. The teacher allows the learner to make choices and decisions, but will challenge if the learner is going off track.

- *Encouraging*. Allowing the learner to make their own decisions, but providing support and encouragement. These learners need to feel through the ILP and action-planning process that they are capable of achieving, as they have the necessary skills but still need a coach to boost their confidence and/or motivation level.

- *Facilitating*. This technique will be most effective with learners in quadrant D. As a technique it involves providing the learner with the resources to complete the task, and allowing them to seek the support needed, possibly through the use of learning contracts, action planning dates and tutorials.

Other coaching models that you may wish to explore further include the GROW model, which follows a sequence of:

G Goal – what are the learners aims?

R Reality – what are the current situation and issues?

O Options – examining solutions, what could you do?

W What – what next?

More information can be found on this model in Whitmore (2002).

So how do coaching and mentoring differ?

Although similar techniques are employed in both coaching and mentoring, and both roles are important within the classroom, there are subtle differences between the two. The main differences can be seen in the table below. The information is taken from http://coachingandmentoring.com/mentsurvey.htm.

Differences between mentoring and coaching

	Mentor	Coach
Focus	Individual	Performance
Role	Facilitator with no agenda	Specific agenda
Relationship	Self-selecting	Comes with the job
Source of influence	Perceived value	Position
Personal returns	Affirmation/learning	Teamwork/performance
Arena	Life	Task related

Coaching, mentoring and counseling

While undertaking the role of tutor, mentor and coach we may find ourselves increasingly in a position where we are providing more than just academic support to our learner and are verging on acting as a counsellor. It is at this stage we need to reconsider whether we are the most appropriate person or whether we now need to signpost to someone more qualified to deal with a specific issue.

'The term 'counselling' includes work with individuals and with relationships which may be developmental, crisis support, psychotherapeutic, guiding or problem solving. The task of counselling is to give the 'client' an opportunity to explore, discover and clarify ways of living more satisfyingly and resourcefully.'

(BAC, 1984, cited in Burnard, 2001)

Research evidence

Carl Rogers (1983) is concerned with student centred, experiential development based upon 'whole person' learning, that is intellectual, emotional and psychological. This is dependent on the creation of an appropriate ethos characterised by friendliness and informality and a spirit of mutuality between teachers and students as participants in learning. The teacher here acts more as a facilitator providing regular and supportive feedback sessions … Rogers' aim is to reduce any threat to the learner's self, so that the student is able to develop the skill to judge the value of the learning experience that has been provided.

Discuss the above in relation to the role of a tutor, mentor, coach and counsellor.

Ethical considerations

Regardless of the role that you choose to adopt with your learners there is a note of caution regarding the ethics surrounding the tutoring/mentoring process.

The following are areas that you should consider when mentoring.

TOP TIP!

Confidentiality

As a tutor and mentor there will be certain discussions that need to remain confidential between you and the learner. However, you also need to be aware of when to involve others, or when to signpost the learner to other areas. For example, if a learner discloses abuse or talks about suicide you need to refer them to professional counsellors, student services or other guidance personnel. Further information on ethics and confidentiality can be found in the suggested reading at the end of the chapter.

Professionalism

Perhaps the most obvious professional roles within mentoring are those in which you are currently working, as teacher, lecturer or tutor. However, within your setting there are also other professionals with whom your learners may have contact, for example, administrative staff or classroom assistants. The most important thing to remember under the ethical consideration of professionalism is that while recognising there are no real clear demarcation lines you will need an understanding of boundaries. Gabriel (2005) defines these boundaries as complex, with the main issues surrounding relationship boundaries. Your setting may have guidelines to follow here.

Equal opportunities

We have all been in a situation where we have had a learner who has been very demanding, requiring constant attention and support. We need to ensure that when mentoring our learners we allow equal access to all and that within such access each individual has equal opportunity and support to that of their peers.

College or school policy and practice

This section would be incomplete without mentioning the need to be aware of your college's or school's policy at all times. What are the guidelines for meeting learners should it be within the normal working day? Can you meet them at the end of the working day? If you are a male teacher working with female learners, what are the regulations surrounding one-to-one meetings?

Why not try this?

Read the guidelines that your workplace has regarding mentoring and tutorial support.

Discuss with your colleagues specific issues that may arise within your tutor/ mentor role and how you should deal with them.

Reflecting on practice

Jo has recently started the diploma in media and is interested in working as a music therapist at a local children's hospice.

He is a fairly confident, outgoing student, although he struggles with some of the more academic aspects of the diploma work. As a result of this he can be very disruptive in your taught classes.

As his tutor you have been asked to mentor him through the more academic challenges of the programme.

Consider the following:

1. What style of mentoring do you think would be most appropriate given the information about this learner?
2. What skills would you need to be able to mentor him effectively?

Conclusion

It is probable that at some stage in your career as a 14–19 teacher you will need to take on the mulit-faceted role of tutor, mentor or counsellor. As a teacher you will need to consider the skills and characteristics that will enable you to mentor effectively. And at all times remember that each learner is different and the approach you take will need to be flexible.

Key ideas summary

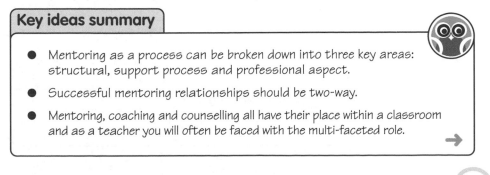

- ● Mentoring as a process can be broken down into three key areas: structural, support process and professional aspect.

- ● Successful mentoring relationships should be two-way.

- ● Mentoring, coaching and counselling all have their place within a classroom and as a teacher you will often be faced with the multi-faceted role.

● You need to be aware of the ethical considerations surrounding the role of mentor and as a teacher should make yourself aware of the organisational guidelines before entering into any mentoring, counselling, coaching role.

Going further

Aldridge, S. and Rigby S. (eds), (2006) *Counselling Skills in Context*, Abingdon: Hodder & Stoughton.

Burnard, P. (2001) *Effective Communication Skills for Health Professionals*, Cheltenham: Nelson Thornes.

Clutterbuck, D. (1985) *Everyone Needs a Mentor*, London: CIPD.

Clutterbuck, D. and Lane, G. (2004) *The Situational Mentor: An International Review of Competences and Capabilities in Mentoring*, Aldershot: Gower.

Darwin, A. (2004) 'Characteristics ascribed to mentors by their protégés', in D. Clutterbuck and G. Lane (eds), *The Situational Mentor: An International Review of Competences and Capabilities in Mentoring*, Aldershot: Gower.

DuBois, D.L. and Karcher M.J. (2005) *Handbook of Youth Mentoring*, Thousand Oaks, CA: Sage.

Gabriel, L. (2005) *Speaking the Unspeakable: The Ethics of Dual Relationships in Counselling*, Hove: Routledge.

Green, M, (2001) *Successful Tutoring: Good Practice for Managers and Tutors*, London: LSDA.

Hohman, R. (2008) *Adult Learner Types*, www.infonet-ae.eu/index.php?option= com_content&task=view&id=381&Itemid=39

Klasen, N. and Clutterbuck, D. (2002) *Implementing Mentoring Schemes: A Practical Guide to Successful Programmes*, Oxford: Butterworth, Heinemann.

Maclennan. N. (1995) *Coaching and Mentoring*, Aldershot: Gower.

Pollard, A. (1997) *Reflective Teaching in the Primary School: A Handbook for the Classroom*, London: Cassell.

Rogers, C. (1983) *Freedom to Learn for the 80s*, Columbus, OH: Merrill.

Whitmore J. (2002) *Coaching For Performance: Growing People, Performance and Purpose*, London: Nicholas Brealey.

http://coachingandmentoring.com/mentsurvey.htm

www.mentors.net

Collaborative working

What this chapter will explore:

- The background and history of collaboration in the 14–19 arena
- Backing to collaborative working
- Advantages and challenges of collaborative working
- Effective partenerships
- Funding and commissioning of provision for 14–19 education

14–19 partnerships are critical in ensuring there is a coherent, locally owned strategy that can provide the 14–19 entitlement for all young people, an entitlement that meets local needs and also has the buy-in of key partners, for example employers.

This chapter will provide you with an overview of the background of collaborative working and will discuss some of the key issues surrounding the establishment of effective partnerships for 14–19 education. There will also be a brief discussion on the new funding and commissioning arrangements for education.

'Collaboration must be focused on the needs of a local learning area rather than simply on the individual needs of one of the partners.'

(Hodgson et al., 2005a, p 1)

The background and history of collaboration in the 14–19 arena

The *14–19 Education and Skills: Implementation Plan* published by the Department for Education and Skills in December 2005 (DfES, 2005) makes it clear that the National Entitlement Curriculum can only be offered through collaborative delivery as no single school will be able to deliver the full entitlement. Instead schools etc. will need to work together in local partnerships with a range of external providers to meet the needs of their students. The process of one or more institution working together in such a way is called collaborative delivery. Collaboration as a process is not a new idea and has been in existence in the British educational system for several years with initiatives such as the 14–19 pathfinder projects and the Increased Flexibility Programme (IFP). However, the Tomlinson report (DfES, 2004) states that for the diploma, 'collaboration would need to happen more systematically if all learners are to have access to a range of options, delivered in institutions with appropriate facilities and expertise'.

Background to collaborative working

The 14–19 Pathfinder Initiative

Pathfinder projects were implemented following the 2002 Green Paper '14–19: Extending Opportunities, Raising Standards' (DfES, 2002) and the government's response '14–19: Opportunity and Excellence' (DfES, 2003). The pathfinders were designed to examine how schools, colleges and work-based learning providers would implement the government agenda of flexibility within the 14–19 curriculum. Twenty-five local authorities were included in the first round of pathfinder projects and a further 14 were successful in the 2003 round. Various initiatives were implemented across the country, for example projects relating to local skills shortages (Derby City Council) and the development of the 14–19 curriculum (Kingswood 14–19 pathfinder project).

Evaluation of the 14–19 pathfinder projects, of which there were 39 across the country, identified 'the positive impact of the continued development of extensive collaborations' (Higham and Yeomans, 2005, p 3) as one of the key findings.

The Increased Flexibility Programme

This programme was introduced in 2002 with the main aim of providing work-related and vocational opportunities for young people and enabled 14–16 year olds to study vocational courses within a post-compulsory setting for part of their school week. The programme was one of the first to embrace widening participation strategies and partnership working (one of the key concepts within the 14–19 framework).

The DfES evaluation of the project highlighted that students choosing to study in further education colleges as part of their education did so because the course reflected a career interest, and that often the institutions were able to offer more specialised resources and expertise. The conclusion of the project was that the partnership working also provided an opportunity for certain students, who may not be suited to school and the learning styles in school, to learn in an alternative environment.

Therefore it can be seen that collaborative delivery as a process has several advantages, including offering wider educational choices for 14–19-year-olds, helping the move from pre- to post-16 learning, and supporting work-based learning. However, collaboration also brings with it several disadvantages and challenges for those involved.

Advantages and challenges of collaborative working

Advantages of collaboration	Disadvantages and challenges of collaboration
Mixed cohorts of learners	Transportation issues
Involvement of employers, HEI to allow easy progression opportunities	Perception of competition amongst providers
Improved access to resources	Monitoring and tracking of learners
Wider range of qualifications	Timetabling
	Staff experiences with 14–16, 16+

Which of the above are likely to impact upon your collaborative working practices? Are there any others that you can add to this list?

As we can see from the table the advantages and the challenges surrounding effective collaborative processes could be daunting for any provider wishing to offer any of the diploma lines, so let us now look at how we can promote collaboration through effective partnership working.

Effective partnerships

The establishment of an effective partnership starts with a shared vision that all of the stakeholders understand and value. This starting point leads to staff and other stakeholders having a degree of ownership and therefore commitment to the overall outcomes. With the diploma lines a shared vision could include:

- offering a broader curriculum;
- making best use of facilities;
- providing access to resources;
- sharing staff expertise and experience;
- ensuring that the national entitlement is in place for all learners.

Why not try this?

Identify the key elements of the shared vision that your organisation would seek to promote amongst its partners. Does it include any of the above suggestions? What other shared vision would be appropriate given the nature of your organisation, its locality and its educational offer?

Essential partnership requirements

The most effective partnerships are comprised of all the key stakeholders within the locality. This could include schools, local colleges, employers, guidance service (such as Connexions), local training providers, local universities, and possibly the voluntary sector.

Reflecting on practice

The following example of partnership working demonstrates how a group of key stakeholders worked together to create an effective modelling tool that has been used to meet the recent government agenda of 14–19, raising the participation age and the introduction of new provision through sixth forms. The information is adapted from DCSF (2009).

City of York

North Yorkshire LSC and York Partnership worked together to develop a curriculum modelling tool in response to the need to plan for the raising of the participation age and the introduction of diplomas, and to accommodate

➡

new provision that came on-line through sixth-form presumptions. The modelling identified that the cohort would be smaller in 2013 than it is now, which made clear that introducing new qualifications would mean a reduced need for existing provision, such as general qualifications, particularly A Levels.

The model was developed to present the scale of change between existing provision and that required for the 14–19 entitlement and the raising of the participation age. The aim was to develop a shared vision for the entitlement across the partnership. The model exemplified simply the issues to be addressed and problems to be resolved and partners were invited to collectively develop a solution. The work was informed by demographic data, current patterns of learner demand, travel to learn, employment and economic data and providers' own projections.

This helped establish a pattern of provision and a rough calculation of learner numbers by provision type, and provided a live model for determining the pattern of provision needed, which allows different factors to be adjusted in order to see the impact that this would have.

Partners in York used this to consider in greater detail what a fixed proportion of learners for diplomas in 2013 would translate into for numbers by line and level. This highlighted the decisions required to make a course viable, including how these relate to the facilities available and how best to achieve economies of scale.

As a result of ongoing promotion and support from the regional adviser through the regional 14–19 network, this has now been explored by every local authority in the Yorkshire and Humber regions, as a tool to help providers visualise the implications of their decisions, and of changes in cohort size and distribution across qualifications. In so doing, it provides a powerful lever for challenging and influencing key partners on the need for collective decisions, in order to create a sustainable mix of provision across the area.

Quality frameworks for partnerships

The DCSF have produced a framework for promoting quality learning within partnerships and providers. Partnerships that wish to demonstrate compliance with this quality framework will need to have the following evidence in place:

A home institution/off-site provider agreement or contract.

Robust disciplinary procedures that are shared, understood and approved by all partners.

A progress report that monitors the progress of individual learners against agreed targets.

An induction procedure with evidence of completion by the individual learner.

Strategies for supporting individual learner need.

A record of current health and safety policy in line with HSE standards covering 14–16 and 16–19 programmes.

Insurance documentation to cover all learners.

Risk assessments to cover all elements of the programme.

A risk assessment of individual learners when appropriate.

A record that all staff involved in learning programmes have been cleared by the Criminal Records Bureau (CRB) for work with children.

Verification that qualifications on offer are listed on Section 96 of the Learning and Skills Act, 2000, and can thus be delivered in Key Stage 4 to learners in the 14–16 age group.

All staff involved in delivery to 14–19-year-olds have received training and/or are working towards a qualification in meeting the needs of this age group.

All staff involved in delivery have received at least basic Safeguarding Board training appropriate to work with young people aged 14-19.

They have a designated Child Protection Coordinator and policies and procedures in place that fulfil Local Safeguarding Board requirements.

They undertake regular surveys of learner experiences.

Suitable documentation and procedures for communication between the home institution and provider to demonstrate an ongoing dialogue regarding the progress of the learner.

The focus of these quality assurance arrangements is to check that programmes:

- meet individual learner needs;
- ensure young people are receiving high standards of education and training;
- inform curriculum planning and staff development strategies;
- offer the learner opportunities for progression;
- provide learners with a suitable and safe learning environment.

(The above list is adapted from DfES (2005).)

Reflecting on practice

Hull and East Riding Partnership

The Hull and East Riding Partnership has been set up to ensure that the schools work in partnership with a range of external providers from the public, private and voluntary sectors to provide an inclusive curriculum which meets the needs of all learners.

In addition the partnership ensures that programmes:

- meet individual learner needs;
- ensure young people are receiving high standards of education and training;
- inform curriculum planning and staff development strategies;
- offer the learner opportunities for progression;
- provide learners with a suitable and safe learning environment.

The partnership itself abides by local agreements that all home institutions and providers comply with current local authority policies, codes of practice, procedures and guidelines for educational visits and off-site activities, although it is the home institution that has the overall responsibility to ensure that they provide a high-quality learning experience both on and off site.

Other aspects of the partnership are that all home institutions and providers have a duty to comply with the Disability Equality Duty and the Race Relations Amendment Act, 2000; and all programmes contribute to the delivery of the *Every Child Matters* outcomes. Each institution or provider is responsible for the quality assurance of its own courses, using its own systems and frameworks of lesson observations, surveys and data analysis and learner surveys and data on retention, attendance, achievement and destinations is collated and shared between all partners.

In relation to quality and inspection, information regarding the quality of provision, e.g. Ofsted inspection reports, external verification reports, Student Perception of Course analyses, should be made available by all partners on request and there is a shared responsibility to ensure that areas of weakness are identified and addressed by all partners.

Consider the following:

Explore the partnership that is in place within your area. Are the elements similar to those described above or do you have other elements in place? What could be improved?

Why not try this?

Make a list of organisations that you will need to partner with to deliver the diploma lines effectively.

How will you ensure that they all play an equal part in the education of the learner?

Funding and commissioning of 14–19 provision

One of the key changes that will take place in 2010 is the funding and commissioning, as opposed to allocation, of education for the 14–19-year-old age group as the control moves from the Learning Skills Councils back to local authorities. From 2010 a National Commissioning Framework (NCF) will be in place to provide support and guidance to all local authorities responsible for commissioning provision, and provision will need to be in secure and established partnerships. New funding bodies and arrangements will also be in place with the introduction of the Young Persons Learning Agency (YPLA), which will have the overall budget for provision.

A typical commissioning decision will be based on the local authority sourcing the provision and making a decision as to the suitability and expertise of the provider, examining areas such as progression, success and inspection grades. The initial decision will be further examined at a regional level before the final decision is communicated to the provider and funding released.

Why not try this?

What are the main considerations that you think the local authority should take into account before making any commissioning decisions?

What do you see as the main issues surrounding commissioning decisions for your organisation?

Conclusion

For the 14–19 agenda and the diploma to be successful there need to be collaborative working practices and partnerships that include all of the stakeholders. Effective collaboration enables effective learning, not just for the learner but for all involved within the 14–19 arena. This will become even more important with the new funding and commissioning processes due to start in 2010.

Key ideas summary

- We need to be aware of the potential issues of working in partnership when entering into agreements.
- We need to consider carefully who we wish to work with.
- There needs to be systems in place to ensure effective partnership working.
- We need strategies to maintain positive employer links.

Going further

DfES (2002) '14–19 Extending Opportunities: Raising Standards', London: DfES.

DfES (2003) '14–19 Opportunity and Excellence', London: DfES.

DfES (2004) *14–19 Curriculum and Qualifications Reform: Final Report of the Working Group on 14–19 Reform*, London: DfES (the Tomlinson Report).

DfES (2005) 14–19 *Education and Skills: Implementation Plan*, DfES: Norwich; and at www.dcsf.gov.uk/14–19/documents/14–19whitepaper.pdf

DfES (2006) *Partnership Guidance*, London: DfES.

DCSF (2009) *14–19 Partnerships and Planning*, London: DfES.

Higham, J. and Yeomans, D. (2005a) *Collaborative Approaches to 14–19 Provision: An Evaluation of the Second Year of the 14–19 Pathfinder Initiative*, London: DfES.

Hodgson, A., Spours, K. and Wright, S. (2005a) *Collaborative Learning Systems*, Nuffield Review of 14–19 Education and Training, Seminar 2, Discussion Paper 10.

Hodgson, A. Spours, K. and Wright, S. (2005b) *The Insitutional Dimension of 14–19 Reform in England: 14–19 Collaborative Learning Systems*, Nuffield Review of 14–19 Education and Training, Discussion Paper 10.

Hodgson, A. Spours, K. and Wright, S. (2005c) *From Collaborative Initiatives to a Coherent 14–19 Phase?*, Nuffield Review of 14–19 Education and Training, Discussion Paper 10; at www.dcsf.gov.uk/14–19/documents

www.dcsf.gov.uk

Possible futures for the 14–19 diploma

As a way of bringing together the previous chapters, this final chapter re-examines some of the issues surrounding the diploma and its introduction into the English educational system against an ever-changing political scene. By the time this book is published it is possible that the UK will have seen a change in government for the first time since 1997 after going to the polls in early 2010. What then could this mean for the diploma and the wider remit of vocational education? Articles in the educational press towards the end of 2009 were extremely scathing about the diploma qualifications and headings along the themes of dumping diplomas were front-page news. Indeed article describes the qualifications as 'flawed' and in some cases 'tantamount to child abuse' (Kelly, 2009). The arguments were based on the ways in which the diplomas have been delivered in some schools and their perceived lack of support within some universities.

There have also been widely documented concerns about the implementation of the qualification itself, and in 2009 the government downscaled the number of learners taking the qualification from 50,000 students to just 12,000, but still insisted that the diploma would be the 'qualification of choice' over GCSE and A levels. The Conservatives say if they win the next general election they will not continue with the academic diploma lines (science, humanities and modern foreign languages) but will instead focus on diplomas becoming high-quality vocational qualifications.

Regardless of these headlines and claims it is my belief, predicated on the success rates of vocational education in other countries, that the concept of the diploma and vocational education is an excellent way in which we can improve skills and routes into employment within the UK. Furthermore, as educators, surely it is our responsibility to ensure that, through both a vocational and an academic agenda, we provide a curriculum that is fit for the future? One that allows learners to choose the route most appropriate for them and therefore meets the needs of all of our young people.

In earlier chapters the following themes were outlined as being key problems and issues surrounding the diploma:

- the vocational/academic divide and the perception that vocational education is subordinate to that of traditional academic education;

- lack of a national system involving all stakeholders in the diploma development, leading to issues of collaboration within consortia;

- levels of employer engagement and the state of the UK economy;

- personalising the learning for each individual and providing the correct motivators for them to succeed;

- training and development needs of the stakeholders involved with the delivery of the vocational qualification;

- the 14–19 sector – where does it sit?

Maybe it is at this juncture that we need to start examining the concept of the diploma and vocational education as a whole, as without a firm home and clear purpose the qualification will remain peripheral to the British educational offering as opposed to being a major player in a comprehensive educational system. This clear lack of natural home and the 14–16/16–19 division has recently been further highlighted with the unveiling of the 'Learning through Life' report, (Schullen and Watson, 2009). This report makes the recommendation that there is a four-stage model for lifelong learning: 18–25, 25–50, 50–75 and 75+. This recommendation, although at the very edge of the 14–19 age bracket, yet again divides the learner population into age brackets that do not seem to sit with the diploma concept and the 14–19 reform agenda. Therefore, do we need to consider a concept that firmly embeds vocational study and the diplomas into the educational system? One that identifies the sector as unique and sets out to achieve education that is 'designed to enhance the skills, knowledge and competencies of individuals … whether these experiences are provided by schools, higher education, private training providers or by employers' (Magalen, 1996, p 3).

What can be determined from the proliferation of policy surrounding 14–19 is that vocational education and the diploma have been 'predicated on the vague but oft-repeated assertion that, politically and culturally, vocational education and training is one of England's main 'historic weaknesses'. Richardson (2007, p 273). However, it can also be argued that the 14–19 concept and the concept of a vocational workforce is not new but a reinvention of several policies over the last few decades (Silver, 1992; Tomlinson, 2001; Neary, 2002).

What is also clear from all of the policy initiatives surrounding the vocational agenda over the last few years is that England, as a country, is still way behind our European counterparts when it comes to the skills agenda. The 2006 White Paper on Further Education ranks the UK 24th out of 29 developed nations in terms of young people staying in education and training post-16 (DfES, 2006). This figure will rise with the raising of the school leaving age to 18 by 2015. However, this will bring its own challenges to the classroom and training arena, although many of these challenges will have been experienced before it has the potential to impact upon the 14–19 classroom, with the possibility of more people opting for vocational programmes, especially if the perception of vocational and academic study continues to suggest that the vocational route is the easier option!

Following the theme of vocational versus academic study, research undertaken in 2004 by Foskett et al. identified the need for post-16 provision to be broad and varied with a good mix of experiential and academic learning. By 2015 this could be translated into not only providing a broad curriculum, but a curriculum fit for all, with a mix of both academic and vocational learning. In addition the provision of training places and apprenticeships with appropriate and willing employers to meet the needs and demands of both the learner population and the economy would greatly benefit the experiential concept.

Hyland and Winch (2007) refer to an imagined Education and Training Act that would go part way in tackling vocational courses and qualifications, proposing:

- the removal of NVQs from mainstream education by 2012 and their return to the workplace;

- all vocational qualifications to include theory underpinning general practice;

- a licence to practise, at a minimum Level 3 for skilled workers.

If this legislation was in place it would move the UK closer to some of the vocational systems in place in Europe, in particular the German system, which has been very effective in removing some of the perceived status of vocational qualifications, and at the same time improving the skill set of the German workforce. Other countries that appear to have challenged the perception of vocational education include Switzerland, where 'two-thirds of young people gain vocational qualifications' (Whitburn, 2003, p 2). A 2009 report in the *Guardian* discusses the present Labour government setting up a new generation of technical schools, sponsored by universities, to train young people in vocational crafts such as engineering and construction (*Guardian*, 2009). The report goes on to suggest that these schools will be called 'university technical colleges' and will be aimed at 14–19 year olds. Some may recognise this concept from the old grammar and technical school era! If this is approved the new colleges will be established as part of the academy programme and they will specialise in a vocational curriculum, delivering the diploma programme with a view to providing a curriculum that, because of its link with the universities, will be highly valued.

This moves us on to other challenges surrounding the qualification, namely the lack of a national system involving all stakeholders in diploma development, leading to issues of collaboration within consortia and the levels of employer engagement. In addition, at the time of writing the UK economy is still in recession and this could potentially have a huge impact on the success or otherwise of the qualifications. First, let us examine the lack of a national system. Apart from two periods in British history, 1964–1973 and 1973–1979, the British government has been reluctant to legislate on the role of employers in vocational education. Some could argue that the 14–19 Implementation Plan (DfES, 2005) is the first attempt to provide such legislation with the introduction of consortia and partnerships to deliver the qualifications. However, much of this is still voluntary, with some employers being more willing to engage than others. Green (1999, p 29) argues that the inclusion of employers will only work when, 'the state defines the roles of others and determines the shape of the system as a whole'. The Ofsted report of 2009, following the introduction of the diplomas, also raises concerns about the lack of collaboration with employers. However, where local employers *were* fully engaged with the qualifications the students were highly motivated. Given that, do we need to consider an Act of Parliament that clearly outlines roles and responsibilities of all stakeholders within the system? Kelly (2009) believes that the British, or more specifically the English, should learn from the French and their new suite of vocational options in the baccalaureat. Additions that have not impacted upon the academic kudos of the qualification, as seems to be the concern in the British educational system.

Let us now consider the kudos of the qualification with the British university system, A BBC report from August 2008 suggests that a large majority of higher education courses in the UK – 80 per cent – will accept the new 14–19 diploma as an entry route (BBC, 2008), but amongst more prestigious research universities in the Russell Group the figure is just 40 per cent, with the caveat that each learner will be treated individually and that in some instances the admissions teams would need to have evidence that the learner had the prerequisite skills and knowledge appropriate for the programme applied for. If this trend is to continue the perceived value of the diploma as a qualification will be greatly reduced in comparison to the more academic routes into university. Here again, do we need to consider some kind of government intervention that ensures equity? After all, on the qualifications framework both A levels and diplomas are Level 3 and therefore should not be treated differently.

Conclusion

It is very difficult to predict what will happen with the diploma over the next few years with the ever-changing political scene. However, regardless of what happens history has shown us that there is a need for a vocational qualification framework within the British system, whether the diploma is the qualification of choice or not. It is also clear that for any vocational qualification to work effectively the government, whoever that may be, needs to implement a system which encourages stakeholders to work together to ensure that we are providing the best education for our young people.

Going further

BBC (2008) 'Most degree courses take diplomas', at
http://news.bbc.co.uk/1/hi/education/8035498.htm

DfES (2005) *14–19 Education and Skills: Implementation Plan*, London: DfES.

DfES (2006) *Further Education: Raising Skills, Improving Life Chance*, London: HMSO.

Foskett, N. Dyke, M. and Maringe, F. (2004) 'The influence of the school in the decision to participate in learning post-16', DfES Research Report.

Green, A. (1999) 'The role of the state and social partners in vocational education and training systems', in T. Hyland and C. Winch (2007), *A Guide to Vocational Education and Training*, New York: Continuum.

Guardian (2009) 'Tory Lord Baker joins goverment on reviving technical schools', at www.guardian.co.uk/politics/2009/aug/government-plans-new technical-schools

Hyland, T. and Winch, C. (2007) *A Guide to Vocational Education and Training*, New York: Continuum.

Kelly, G. (2009) 'Vocational debate won't die with jinxed diploma', *The Times Educational Supplement*, 11 September.

Magalen, L. (1996) 'VET and the university', Inaugural Professorial Lecture, Dept of Vocational Education and Training, University of Melbourne.

Neary, M. (2002) *Curriculum Studies in Post-compulsory and Adult Education*, Cheltenham: Nelson Thornes.

Richardson, W. (2007) 'Perspectives on vocational education and training in post-war England', *Journal of Vocational Education & Training*, 59, 3, 273–7.

Schullen, T. and Watson, D. (2009) *Learning through Life: An Enquiry into the Future for Lifelong Learning*, Leicester: NIACE.

Silver, H. (1992) 'Knowing and not knowing in the history of education', *History of Education*, 21, 1, 105.

Tomlinson, S. (2001) *Education in a Post-welfare Society*, Buckingham: Open University Press.

Whitburn, J. (2003) 'Motivating 14–16 years olds: How do the Swiss do it?', draft paper presented at the ESRC-funded seminar series 'How to motivate (demotivated) 14–16 years olds with special reference to work related education and training', 14 February.

www.fefocus.co.uk

Appendix 1
MCBER'S THREE MEASURES OF TEACHER EFFECTIVENESS

Measure	Personal evaluation	Area for development
Teaching skills		
High expectations		
Planning		
Teaching methods and strategies		
Behaviour management and discipline		
Time and resource management		
Assessment		
Setting of independent task (homework)		
Professional characteristics		
Professionalism: Respect for others Challenge and support Confidence		
Planning and setting expectations: Improvement drive Information seeking (students) Initiative		

Measure	Personal evaluation	Area for development
Analytical thinking skills		
Relating to others: Understanding Impact and influence Team working		
Leading: Managing learning and learners Passion Flexibility Holding people accountable (allowing independent learning		
Classroom climate		
Clarity of task		
Logical order and progression		
Standards		
Interest		
Learner safety		
Support for learners		
Fairness		

Source: Hay McBer (2000) *Research into Teacher Effectiveness*, Report by Hay McBer to the Department for Education and Employment, Hay Group/DfEE. Reprinted with permission.

Appendix 2

GARDNER'S MULTIPLE INTELLIGENCE TYPES AND CHARACTERISTICS WITH POSSIBLE ACTIVITIES FOR USE WITHIN DIPLOMA TEACHING

	Intelligence type	Description	Possible diploma tasks, activities or tests
1	**Linguistic**	These learners like using words, often auditory learners, or very high auditory skills. Can be taught through imagery.	Complete word searches or crosswords. Develop a photo album showing a specific topic within their subject area. Provide a written set of instructions on how to complete a particular task, e.g. how to make a cake (hospitality), journey details for a holiday (travel) or how to create a chart in an Excel spreadsheet (IT). Develop a video on a given topic within the diploma subject area in which students give short talks.
2	**Logical Mathematical**	These learners are good at problem solving and puzzles.	Tasks involving mystery solving, e.g. 'who dunnit' games – to develop PLTS and functional skills. Develop an action plan that will enable them to solve a particular task with specific aims and objectives. Complete a costing for an event that the learners will complete. Complete a written assessment/rationale for a proposed project.

	Intelligence type	Description	Possible diploma tasks, activities or tests
3	**Musical**	These learners not only enjoy music but are responsive to noise in the learning environment.	Develop a 'rap' or similar to remember a specific subject. Set work to lyrics. Decide on background music for given events/situations that will take place within the subject area, e.g. hotel lobby for hospitality. Make use of multimedia within the classroom.
4	**Bodily–Kinesthetic**	These learners like movement and building things.	Demonstrate a movement linked to the diploma line, e.g. a sport activity. Act out scenarios, role play, use of hands-on activities within the classroom.
5	**Spatial–Visual**	These learners are aware of the environment around them.	Create a poster as a learning activity. Create a room layout for an event. Design a logo for a new company within their subject area. Develop a scrapbook of learning.
6	**Interpersonal**	Students learn through interaction with others.	Roleplay using body language and facial expressions to show feeling. Telephone roleplay, use of email/facebook/twitter/blogs in learning circles.
7	**Intrapersonal**	These are independent learners and tend to work well by themselves.	Create and review an individual learning plan with specific aims and objectives. Reflect on own learning through a reflective journal.

(The Intelligence types listed above are taken from Gardner, H. (2003) *Multiple Intelligences: The Theory in Practice*, New York: Basic Books.)

Appendix 3

POSSIBLE QUALIFICATIONS FOR ASSESSMENT

Assessor Role	Possible Qualifications
Teacher assessor	D32, D33 A1, A2
Internal verifier	D34, D36 V1, V2
External verifier	D35

Appendix 4
INDIVIDUAL LEARNING PLAN EXAMPLES

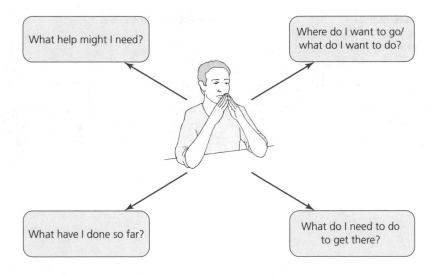

What help might I need?

Where do I want to go/ what do I want to do?

What have I done so far?

What do I need to do to get there?

Individual Learning Plan – Initial Assessment 1
Previous Achievement Record

Name:	1st Review date:
Tutor	2nd Review date:

Course/Level achieved in GCSE English and maths or equivalent

Subject-specific qualifications to be taken

I would like to get these results

Career aspirations/Progression goals

I would like to work as/in

I would like to do further study at

Work experience/Previous posts

I have a part-time job in

Medical history
I would like to achieve these goals and targets (e.g. target grades for qualifications)
I would like to take part in these wider activities
Personal statement – indicating strengths and areas to be improved and aspirations

Individual Learning Plan – Initial Assessment 2
Initial Skills and Abilities Self-assessment

Please indicate, using the 0–10 scale (0 no ability/confidence, 10 very able/confident), your current level of ability/confidence in the following areas.

Skill/ability	Assessment level										
1. Writing assignments	0	1	2	3	4	5	6	7	8	9	10
2. Delivering presentations	0	1	2	3	4	5	6	7	8	9	10
3. Working on your own	0	1	2	3	4	5	6	7	8	9	10
4. Working in a group	0	1	2	3	4	5	6	7	8	9	10
5. Researching a topic	0	1	2	3	4	5	6	7	8	9	10
6. Using IT-Word documents	0	1	2	3	4	5	6	7	8	9	10
7. Using Access, Excel, the internet etc.	0	1	2	3	4	5	6	7	8	9	10
8. Using the Internet to research	0	1	2	3	4	5	6	7	8	9	10
9. Planning your time effectively	0	1	2	3	4	5	6	7	8	9	10
10. Meeting deadlines	0	1	2	3	4	5	6	7	8	9	10
11. Asking for support, if you need it	0	1	2	3	4	5	6	7	8	9	10
12. Working with a mentor/tutor	0	1	2	3	4	5	6	7	8	9	10
Total score as a percentage	$\dfrac{\text{Total score}}{120} \times 100 =$										

Learning styles – what's yours?

This chart helps you determine your learning style. Read the word in the left column and then answer the questions in the successive three columns to see how you respond to each situation. Your answers may fall into all three columns, but one column is likely contain the most answers. The dominant column indicates your primary learning style.

When you ...	Visual	Auditory	Kinaesthetic & Tactile
Spell	Do you try to see the word?	Do you sound out the word or use a phonetic approach?	Do you write the word down to find if it feels right?
Talk	Do you sparingly but dislike listening for too long? Do you favour words such as *see, picture* and *imagine*?	Do you enjoy listening but are impatient to talk? Do you use words such as *hear, tune* and *think*?	Do you gesture and use expressive movements? Do you use words such as *feel, touch* and *hold*?
Concentrate	Do you become distracted by untidiness or movement?	Do you become distracted by sounds or noises?	Do you become distracted by activity around you?
Meet someone again	Do you forget names but remember faces or remember where you met?	Do you forget faces but remember names or remember what you talked about?	Do you remember best what you did together?
Contact people on business	Do you prefer direct, face-to-face, personal meetings?	Do you prefer the telephone?	Do you talk with them while walking or participating in an activity?
Read	Do you like descriptive scenes or pause to imagine the actions?	Do you enjoy dialogue and conversation or hear the characters talk?	Do you prefer action stories or are not a keen reader?
Do some-thing new at work	Do you like to see demonstrations, diagrams, slides or posters?	Do you prefer verbal instructions or talking about it with someone else?	Do you prefer to jump right in and try it?
Put something together	Do you look at the directions and the picture?		Do you ignore the directions and figure it out as you go along?
Need help with a computer application	Do you seek out pictures or diagrams?	Do you call the help desk, ask a neighbour, or growl at the computer?	Do you keep trying to do it or try it on another computer?
Total score			

Source: Adapted from Rose, C. and Nicholl, M. J. (1987) *Accelerated Learning for the 21st Century*, New York: Dell. Reprinted with permission.

Your own VAK learning style–tips

Learning style	Preferred learning	Strategies
Visual learner	Prefer information to be presented visually, in picture or design format. You like teachers to use visual aids, video, maps, charts. You prefer books with pictures and diagrams. You prefer a quiet learning environment, and dislike group work. You visualise your work, and may be artistic.	• Flashcards, with pictures • Use margins to add symbols/pictures • Highlighter pens for key words/ colour code • Use charts to organise information • Use graph paper to structure work • Use the PC to organise/structure your work
Auditory learner	Prefer information in an oral language format. Enjoy formal lectures and group discussions. Can learn from audio tapes. When thinking about learning remember in 'words' Learn best working with others in discussion.	• Study group work • Speak out loud to revise • Tape-record your lectures • Create your own 'study tapes' • Talk your way through problems, e.g. in science or maths
Kinaesthetic Learner	Prefer 'hands-on learning', like to manipulate models/materials to learn. Enjoy demonstrations, fieldwork, class activities.	• Sit near the front, take notes • Use key words, charts and pictures • Don't worry about spellings, etc, in your own notes • Walk up and down as you read to learn • Draw models, flow charts to structure learning • Use flash cards and sequence them to check learning • Limit the information on each card to a word or picture • Colour code with highlighters • Use the PC to introduce movement to your learning in terms of typing

Summary of Initial/Summative Assessment

Category	Initial score	Final score	Distance travelled
Initial skills and abilities Literacy score Numeracy score **Total**			
Learning styles Visual Auditory Kinaesthetic			

Personal targets for programme

Teaching experience	
Initial skills and abilities	
Literacy **Numeracy**	

	Name (print)	Signature
Student		
Teacher		

Example Action Plan

Action Planning to Meet Individual Skills Needs

Area for development	Specific *What is it?*	Measurable *How will you measure it?*	Achievable *Realistically by when?*	Realistic *Is it a reasonable target?*	Time bound *When will you have achieved this?*	Evaluated *How did it go?*	Reviewed *Did it work?*

Index

Page numbers in *italics* denotes a diagram/figure

Classroom Gems

Innovative resources, inspiring creativity across the school curriculum

Designed with busy teachers in mind, the Classroom Gems series draws together an extensive selection of practical, tried-and-tested, off-the-shelf ideas, games and activities, guaranteed to transform any lesson or classroom in an instant.

Games and activities for
Primary Modern Foreign Languages
Nicola Davenport

© 2008 Paperback 336pp
ISBN: 9781405873925

Practical ideas, games and activities for the
Primary Classroom
Paul Barron

© 2008 Paperback 312pp
ISBN: 9781405859455

Games, ideas and activities for
Primary PE
Will Allen

© 2009 Paperback 224pp
ISBN: 9781408220382

Games, ideas and activities for
Learning Outside the Primary Classroom
Paul Barron

© 2009 Paperback 256pp
ISBN: 9781408225608

Games, ideas and activities for
Primary Mathematics
John Dabell

© 2009 Paperback 304pp
ISBN: 9781408223208

Games, ideas and activities for
Primary Humanities
Richard Green

© 2009 Paperback 304pp
ISBN: 9781408228098

Games, ideas and activities for
Primary Music
Donna Minto

© 2009 Paperback 304pp
ISBN: 9781408223260

Games, ideas and activities for
Primary Drama
Michael Theodorou

© 2009 Paperback 304pp
ISBN: 9781408223291

Games, ideas and activities for
Early Years Phonics
Lynn Cousins and Gill Coulson

© 2009 Paperback 304pp
ISBN: 9781408224359

Creative activities for the
Secondary Classroom
Mark Labrow

© 2009 Paperback 256pp
ISBN: 9781408225578

Games, ideas and activities for
Primary Science
John Dabell

© 2010 Paperback 304pp
ISBN: 9781408223239

Games, ideas and activities for
Primary Literacy
Hazel Glynne and Amanda Snowden

© 2010 Paperback 336pp
ISBN: 9781408225516

'Easily navigable, allowing teachers to choose the right activity quickly and easily, these invaluable resources are guaranteed to save time and are a must-have tool to plan, prepare and deliver first-rate lessons'

Longman is an imprint of

PEARSON

The Essential Guides Series

Practical skills for teachers

The Essential Guides series offers a wealth of practical support, inspiration and guidance for NQTs and more experienced teachers ready to implement into their classroom. The books provide practical advice and tips on the core aspects of teaching and everyday classroom issues, such as planning, assessment, behaviour and ICT. The Essential Guides are invaluable resources that will help teachers to successfully navigate the challenges of the profession.

Longman is an imprint of

PEARSON

Practical skills for teachers